AMY ROBSART

Also by Christine Hartweg

John Dudley:
The Life of Lady Jane Grey's Father-in-Law

Christine Hartweg

AMY ROBSART

A Life and Its End

Amy Robsart

A Life and Its End

First published in 2017

Copyright © 2017 Christine Hartweg

All rights reserved.
No part of this publication may be reproduced or transmitted in any form or by any means without prior permission of the author.

ISBN 978-1548783600

Cover photo: Detail of *Eleonora di Toledo*, c.1560, by Agnolo Bronzino.
Courtesy The National Gallery of Art, Washington

Author's address: Königsweg 208 f, 14129 Berlin, Germany
e-mail: allthingsrd@t-online.de

http://www.allthingsrobertdudley.wordpress.com

Contents

   Introduction 7
1 A Norfolk Girl 11
2 A Favourite's Wife 28
3 My Wife is Dead 46
4 Accident? 62
5 Suicide? 75
6 Dishonourable Reports 80
7 Murder? 94
8 Old Boys 113
9 Epilogue 134
   Bibliography 146
   Index 153

INTRODUCTION

Amy Dudley *née* Robsart is best known for falling down the stairs. She was the first wife of Robert Dudley, later Earl of Leicester, the favourite and great love of Queen Elizabeth I. Elizabeth came to the English throne in November 1558, and her interest in Robert was observed soon afterwards. Amy died, aged 28, in what is usually called mysterious circumstances on 8 September 1560 at her lodgings at Cumnor Place, near Abingdon, Oxfordshire.

Her death was certainly unusual and was seen as such at the time. It was judged an accident by the coroner's jury, but there were many people who believed it was murder and there were some who believed it was suicide. Her husband may have been one of the latter.

The circumstances of Amy's death can be reconstructed, to a certain extent, from a set of contemporary letters as well as from the recently found coroner's report of her case. Many more supposed details have been, and are still added, to the story. They often come from popular novels and regularly pop up in both non-fiction books and forums such as Facebook. They usually concern Amy's clothing: She is supposed to have worn a nightgown, her hood is supposed to have had no blood on it and, most famously, her hood supposedly did not move from its position during her supposed murder.

There are also more subtle misconceptions. For example, the timing of her death is often described as very convenient, and too convenient to be coincidental; however, one might ask why, if she was murdered, she was not dispatched a lot earlier. Amy Dudley died no less than 22 months – almost two years – after Elizabeth's accession (and the queen's infatuation with her Master of the Horse started almost immediately). The question is how long into Elizabeth's reign should Amy have died so as not to arouse suspicion? Three years, four years, five years? Perhaps ten years.

Other possible misconceptions concern Amy Dudley's character, about which we know hardly anything. She likely was a beautiful young woman with good manners, in short, a very nice person. It is unlikely that she was a shrew. It is equally unlikely though that she was the demure, tragic heroine of historical fiction. Likewise, there is very little evidence that would prove that Robert Dudley treated his wife badly; from early 1559 he was in an impossible situation where his marriage was concerned, and there is evidence that Elizabeth did not look friendly on the fact that he had a wife.

*

I became fascinated with Amy Robsart through my interest in Robert Dudley, and I have aimed to tell her life story based on the available sources, a few of which have not been used in earlier accounts. I will also, of course, discuss her death and its possible causes, as well as the later occurrences connected with it in the lives of Amy's widower and other people. We will for the first time have an in-depth look into the person and background of her supposed killer, Sir Richard Verney, and also discuss the possible involvement of William Cecil in her death.

There will always remain some doubts as to how or by whose hand Amy Dudley died in September 1560. It has been argued that her death changed English history. And it is my personal conviction that if she was murdered this would have had even greater repercussions; especially on the lives of the surviving protagonists, her killers included. I am therefore inclined to believe it was an accident or possibly suicide that killed her. As will be shown, there are also misconceptions about the possibility of fatal stair accidents, as well as 16th century suicides.

Figure 1: Portrait miniature of an unknown lady, c.1550. It has been suggested that she might be Amy Robsart. (Courtesy Yale Center for British Art).

ONE

A NORFOLK GIRL

On 7 June 1532 the Norfolk gentleman, Sir John Robsart, made a note in his prayerbook. It said, in Latin, that Amy Robsart, his "beloved daughter", was born on this day. Sir John had married Amy's mother, Elizabeth Appleyard *née* Scott, in 1530. Amy was his only legitimate child; she had, however, an illegitimate half-brother, Arthur Robsart. Amy also had four half-siblings from her mother's previous marriage: John, Philip, Anne, and Frances Appleyard.[1]

The Robsarts descended from Chanoine de Robersart, a knight from Hainault who had come to England in the 1360s during the Hundred Years War.[2] Sir John Robsart of Syderstone was a substantial country gentleman. From 1532 he regularly served as one of Norfolk's JPs and he was the proud owner of three manors and 3,000 sheep.[3]

Amy almost certainly grew up at her mother's house, Stanfield Hall, as Syderstone was not in a state to be lived in. Stanfield manor, whose history went back to Anglo-Saxon times, bordered on the market town of Wymondham. Like her future husband, Robert Dudley, Amy Robsart grew up in an atmosphere of religious reform. In 1550 the preacher Thomas Becon dedicated a book to her father, writing of the "godly affection and christian zeal which both you ... and your wife have borne toward the pure religion of God these

---
1 Skidmore 2010 p. 15
2 Tuchman 1979 p. 302
3 Skidmore 2010 p. 15

many years."[1] Amy received a good education and wrote in a fine hand.[2]

John Robsart's Appleyard stepchildren all married into respectable Norfolk families: The Bigots, the Huggins, the Sheltons, and the Flowerdews. Sir John Flowerdew, a lawyer and the father-in-law of Amy's sister Frances Appleyard, also worked as John Robsart's steward. Unfortunately, he had been quarrelling with Robert Kett, another Norfolk landowner, for many years. Robert Kett, in his turn, was Elizabeth Robsart's brother-in-law, from her previous marriage to Roger Appleyard. The quarrel had been about the enclosing of some common land on the part of John Flowerdew. When, in the early summer of 1549, Flowerdew offered to pay 3s 4d for the pulling down of the hedges of Robert Kett, Kett decided to do just that himself, as well as leading the people of Norfolk into rebellion against "importunate lords".[3]

In August 1549, the government of Protector Somerset sent an army to deal with the uprisings, after all the rebels were by then holding the town of Norwich, England's second largest city at the time. A first attempt to "liberate" Norwich went totally wrong and Somerset was obliged to send a second, larger army under John Dudley, Earl of Warwick, one of the most powerful men in the country.

On 22 August his forces arrived at Wymondham, where the officers were logded in Sir John Robsart's house.[4] Among the overnight guests were Warwick's sons, Ambrose and Robert Dudley. The young men were about 18 and 17 years old, respectively, and both were "going to the wars" for the first time.

---

1 Skidmore 2010 p. 16
2 Skidmore 2010 p. 17
3 Skidmore 2010 pp. 15–16
4 Holinshed IV 1.21.1.; Skidmore 2010 p. 14

Three days before her 18th birthday in June 1550, Amy Robsart married Robert Dudley. They were almost exactly of the same age, and probably met when the royal army had camped on the grounds of Sir John Robsart's estate in August 1549.[1] On 20 May 1550 Sir John Robsart and John Dudley, Earl of Warwick, agreed on a marriage contract for their children – if the "said Robert and Amye will thereunto condescend and agree".[2] It seems they did, for William Cecil, a likely wedding guest, later remarked that the union of Amy and Robert had been a "carnal marriage", beginning in joy and ending in mourning.[3] That the 17-year-old Robert fell in love with his host's 17-year-old daughter is probably the best explanation for this son of England's chief minister to marry the heiress of an influential country gentleman.

The wedding took place on 4 June 1550 at the former royal palace of Sheen, a day after the much grander nuptials of Robert Dudley's eldest brother, John, with the eldest daughter of the Duke of Somerset, Anne. Anne was considerably younger than her husband, and also than Amy. This match was entirely political, for Somerset and Warwick were old friends but also political rivals. A few weeks after the rebellion in Norfolk, Robert's father, the Earl of Warwick, had led a coup against the Lord Protector, who was removed from office and imprisoned. He was soon released from the Tower, however, on Warwick's initiative,[4] and the wedding

---
1 Wilson 1981 pp. 33, 43. It is sometimes said that Robert Dudley was born in 1533, and the Elizabethan historian William Camden even implied that Robert was born on the same day as Elizabeth I. This is however contradicted by a letter in which Robert named 24 June as his birthday. From a description on a miniature by Nicholas Hilliard it is possible to calculate the year of his birth (Adams 2008b).
2 Skidmore 2010 pp. 23–24
3 Wilson 1981 p. 189; Adams 2011
4 Adams, Archer, Bernard 2003a p. 135

13

between their children was intended to symbolize renewed amity between them. The 12-year-old King Edward, the bride's cousin, was present at the festivities and greatly amused himself, writing down everything in his journal. Edward watched mock battles and masques, and there was "a fair dinner made", a great banquet. The next day, Edward noted,

> Sir Robert Dudeley, third sonne to th'erle of Warwic, maried sir Jon Robsartes daughter, after wich mariage ther were certain gentlemen that did strive who shuld first take away a gose's heade, wich was hanged alive on tow crose postes.[1]

Notably absent from such rumbustious pleasures was the Earl of Warwick, Amy's father-in-law, who, it was believed, was either sick or feared to be poisoned.[2]

Robert's match cannot have been particularly attractive for the elder John Dudley, though he was certainly happy to acquire a relative in John Robsart and thus influence in a troubled area of England. John Dudley and John Robsart had agreed that the young couple would only inherit the Robsart estate after the death of both of Amy's parents, not just her father, as would have been the norm. Furthermore, the earl paid £200 as a "dowry" for Robert to Sir John, who in his turn was to pay his son-in-law £20 p.a. From his father, Robert received a rent of £50 p.a., as well as the former priory of Coxford, which lay near the Robsart estate. To this John Dudley later added two manors, near Holt and near Great Yarmouth, so that "his son might be able to keep a good house in Norfolk".[3] – "Know ye that I have given and

---

1 Literary Remains II p. 273–275
2 Adams, Archer, Bernard 2003b p. 52
3 Skidmore 2010 p. 24

granted the said manor, etc., to Robert Dudley, Lord Dudley, my son and the Ladie Amie his wife."[1]

During the next few years, Robert Dudley served as a member of parliament as well as in local offices alongside his father-in-law. He thus gained the respect of the Norfolk gentry, lasting well into the Elizabethan era: "[Y]our Lordship's name is in Norfolk of some authority and your person well beloved" was the opinion of Bishop John Aylmer.[2]

But Amy and her husband did not just live in the country, in fact they seem mostly to have resided in the capital, at Ely Place, the town residence of the Duke and Duchess of Northumberland, as Robert's parents were since October 1551. In the same month of October 1551, the Duke of Somerset was arrested and the political drama ended with his execution on a cold morning in January 1552. Anne Seymour, Amy's young sister-in-law who was now orphaned, continued to live in the Dudley household, so if Amy had any contact with her nothing much would have changed.

As the son of a duke, Robert was now to be called "Lord Robert" and became the proud holder of two court offices, Chief Carver and Master of the Buckhounds. From August 1551 he was also a gentleman of Edward VI's privy chamber.[3] Amy, however, would not have spent any time there. The court of a young, unmarried king was a male-dominated affair and access was strictly controlled. In December 1552 Robert was appointed keeper of Somerset House, which had been granted to the Lady Elizabeth, Henry VIII's younger daughter. The former residence of the recently executed Edward Seymour, Duke of Somerset, was a great Renaissance palace and still a building site. That is probably

---

1 Jackson 1878 p. 84
2 Skidmore 2010 p. 24
3 Adams 2008b

why Elizabeth never visited the place, but at least Amy and Robert had now a London residence of their own.[1]

This agreeable life ended with the death of Edward VI on 6 July 1553. The 15-year-old Edward had died after a long consumptive illness, and during the last months of the king's life the atmosphere at court must have become rather gloomy. On 25 May Amy had probably witnessed the magnificent wedding celebrations of her 16-year-old brother-in-law, Guildford, with Lady Jane Grey, daughter of the Duke of Suffolk. Lady Jane, also 16, was of the blood royal, the king's first cousin once removed, and Edward was about to appoint her as heir, excluding his two half-sisters, Mary and Elizabeth, from the succession. Jane was a committed Protestant like himself.

She was proclaimed queen on 10 July 1553 at the Tower of London amid official festivities, but the public response was remarkably muted. Immediately after Edward's death, Robert Dudley had been sent by his father with a small army to East Anglia in order to arrest Mary. Amy remained behind, either with the court or possibly at Somerset House. The atmosphere among both councillors and ladies at the Tower was very tense and turned into despair when Mary sent a letter in which she demanded to be acknowledged as the rightful queen. It was decided that the Duke of Northumberland should lead a bigger army to East Anglia.

Jane's reign continued for almost another week until on 19 July the majority of councillors changed sides and proclaimed Mary. Amy would have witnessed Londoners "mad with joy" banqueting in the streets, as well as bonfires and two days and nights of bell-ringing.[2] Her mood would not have been like partying, however, after all she did not know what had become of her husband, nor would she have been thrilled by the prospect of a Catholic monarch. Jane was

---

1   Adams 2008b
2   Whitelock 2009 p. 174

moved from her state apartments into her prison quarters, while Amy's mother-in-law and her brother-in-law Guildford were likewise locked up in the Tower. Her father-in-law and other brothers-in-law were escorted through London a few days later; they were much reviled by the populace, but there was still no trace of Robert.[1]

Robert Dudley had been campaigning for nearly a fortnight when he was arrested at King's Lynn on the 20th, having taken the town and proclaimed Queen Jane only the day before. The next day he found himself a prisoner at Framlingham Castle, Mary's headquarters, and on 26 July he also arrived at the Tower.[2] Meanwhile, the Duchess of Northumberland had already been released and it seems likely that Amy moved in with her mother-in-law, as she would hardly have been allowed to stay in the palatial Somerset House any longer. The duchess was later known to reside in a house at Chelsea, and Amy may also have found a temporary home in the house of her sister-in-law Mary Sidney, the eldest of the Duke of Northumberland's daughters. Mary had been chosen to escort Lady Jane to Syon House, the place where Jane was to be informed that she was now queen, and in 1551 had married the courtier Henry Sidney for love.[3] A year later the Sidneys had been granted Penshurst Place in Kent, which now became a retreat for beleaguered Dudley family members.

On 22 August the Duke of Northumberland was executed, and about this time Mary's council issued a warrant to a clerk of the Exchequer,

> to deliver ... such stuff, apparel and other things as he hath got into his hands of the Lord Robert Dudley's, unto the lady his wife, and the same

---

1 Greyfriars Chronicle pp. 80–81
2 Haynes 1987 pp. 23–24; Greyfriars Chronicle p. 81
3 Hartweg 2016 pp. 108–109

being called for her after, to be always answerable for their forthcoming to the Queen's Highness' use.[1]

Amy indeed gave up stuffs to the vice-chamberlain of the royal household, for he received a letter concerning "such apparel and other things as he hath of the Lady Dudley's, the Lord Robert's wife."[2] Robert and his four brothers were lodged in a room in the Beauchamp Tower. Before mid-September the Lieutenant of the Tower received a council order that willed him

> to permit these ladies following to have access unto their husbands, and there to tarry with them so long and at such times as by him shall be thought meet; that is to say, the Lord Ambrose's wife, the Lord Robert's wife, Sir Francis Jobson's wife, Sir Harry Gates's wife and Sir Richard Corbett's wife.[3]

Procreation being a chief duty of mankind, and of married couples in an age of high child mortality, marital sex was not easily denied to prisoners;[4] and so, three of the Dudley brothers were granted visits from their wives. It is quite possible that Amy would have met her sisters-in-law, Anne, Countess of Warwick, and Elizabeth, Lady Tailboys, who was Ambrose Dudley's wife, at the Tower.

Also in September, Amy's husband was scheduled for attainder by parliament, but proceedings dragged on and were put aside. Then, on 13 November 1553, Robert's

---

1 APC IV p. 323
2 APC IV p. 328
3 APC IV p. 344
4 Even Catholic wives imprisoned for their religion in Elizabethan England were periodically allowed to go home so that their husbands were not deprived of their marital services (Fraser 1996 p. 28).

brothers Ambrose, Guildford, and Henry were "led out of the Tower on foot," to be arraigned at the Guildhall, "with the axe before them". They were all convicted of treason, alongside Guildford's wife, Lady Jane, and "Doctor Cranmer, Archbishop of Canterbury".[1] There was still hope for pardon. The situation escalated in January, when a major rebellion broke out against Queen Mary's plans to marry Philip of Spain. Guildford and Jane were executed within less than three weeks, shortly after the defeat of Thomas Wyatt before the gates of London on 3 February. Amy may have witnessed some of these events through her visits to the Beauchamp Tower, after all the prisoners were well positioned to oversee the battle. She would have been even more agitated by the arraignment of Robert, likewise at Guildhall, on 22 January 1554. He was condemned the next day, but so far not attainted.[2] The couple could keep their few possessions for the time being.

The influx of Spanish courtiers in the summer of 1554 brought more opportunities for Robert's mother to lobby for her sons' release. Philip of Spain, now Mary's consort and co-ruler, saw the need to make as many friends as possible among the English nobility and lent a sympathetic ear. In October 1554 Robert and his brothers John and Henry came free. Ambrose still had to stay behind for about a month. This was because he was expected to be the family heir in a matter of days, for John, Amy's eldest brother-in-law, was dying. The young Earl of Warwick indeed died three days after his release from the Tower, at Penshurst, the house of his brother-in-law Henry Sidney.[3] There were now only three brothers left.

In the meantime, in June 1554, Sir John Robsart had also died. His property went to his widow, Amy's mother, as had

---

1 Chronicle of Queen Jane p. 32; Machyn p. 48
2 Adams 2008b
3 Adams 2008b; Machyn p. 72

been stipulated in Amy's marriage contract. Shortly after his release, Robert Dudley was finally attainted by parliament, which meant that he officially lost whatever he possessed and his right of inheritance also. Thus, Amy and Robert were in a precarious financial situation, more so than either Ambrose or Henry Dudley, who had both married wealthy ladies. In the event, John Appleyard, Amy's half-brother, seems to have supported Robert and Amy.[1] Amy's mother-in-law died in January 1555 and left her children some property, which after a couple of months the queen graciously allowed them to inherit, despite the attainder.[2] The widowed Duchess of Northumberland had made many friends among the Spanish nobles who had come with King Philip. The Duchess of Alba, wife to the famous general, was one such and was asked "to continue a good lady to all [my] children as she has begun". To her Jane Dudley left her green parrot; to Amy she left "a gown of wrought velvet". Robert received 50 marks from his mother, as did Henry, his youngest brother, who was not older than 15 or 16. Her youngest daughter Katherine, a child of not yet 12, also received 50 marks. The manor of Hales Owen, a former monastery, went to Ambrose Dudley, along with 100 marks. Her eldest daughter, Mary Sidney, received much more: 200 marks and the most precious household stuff, like tapestries, as well as personal keepsakes.[3]

Ambrose and Robert soon had occasion to resume a familiar sport: they took part in a series of tournaments held in January 1555, as King Philip was celebrating Anglo-Spanish friendship. At this time the three brothers were also formally pardoned, the attainder remaining in force, though.[4] Despite the demonstrations of royal clemency, the Dudley

---

1 HMC Salisbury I p. 350
2 Adams 2002 p. 159
3 Collins 1745 p. 34; Hartweg 2016 p. 20
4 Adams 2008b

brothers were not exactly welcome at the court or in London; during the queen's "confinement" (or phantom pregnancy) they were ordered to leave the city – they had been seen at St. Paul's Cathedral in the company of "known malcontents". In April 1556, after another anti-government conspiracy, by the Dudley brothers' distant cousin, Sir Henry Dudley, the French ambassador reported that "the children of the Duke of Northumberland are all on the run and great efforts are being made to apprehend them".[1] It is true that a number of Dudley associates were in trouble, although nothing more specific is known about Robert and his brothers. Certainly, Amy Dudley's situation cannot have been too comfortable.

Her financial situation had improved, though. In November 1555 Ambrose, Henry, and their uncle, Sir Andrew Dudley, had come to the conclusion that Robert was "left with nothing to live by ... having most need of friendly and brotherly love".[2] Robert should now have Hales Owen on condition that he pay his mother's debts and grant his sister Katherine a rent of 50 marks p.a. Ambrose and Andrew Dudley were each to receive £800 from him, while Henry, married to a rich wife, did not demand anything.[3] Henry's wife Margaret's great London house, the former Augustinian priory known as Christchurch, was a most welcome home for Robert and Amy; they were still using it in the late 1550s, when Margaret had remarried and was the Duchess of Norfolk.[4]

*

The year 1557 started very well, for Robert was among the

---
1 My translation from Adams 2002 p. 161: "les enfans du duc de Northumberland sont tous fugitifs et que l'on a fait une grande diligence pour les prendre".
2 Adams 2002 p. 159
3 Adams 2002 pp. 171, 159
4 Adams 1995 pp. 43, 378

persons considered worthy to exchange New Year gifts with Queen Mary.[1] Amy was now almost a courtier's wife again. In March, Robert was at Calais with a military mission led by the Earl of Pembroke. The contingent was awaiting Philip's return to England and Robert was sent ahead to bring the happy news to Queen Mary:[2]

> The xvij day of Marche cam rydyng from kyng Phelype from be-yond the see unto the court at Grenwyche, to owre quen, with letters in post, my lord Robart Dudley, ... that the kyng wold com to Cales the xvij day of Marche.[3]

In June 1557, Amy's mother also died. Amy and Robert could now take over the 3,000 Robsart sheep and start clearing debts. They could not move into Syderstone manor, however, as it was still as uninhabitable as it had been in Amy's childhood. When not in London, they were now apparently living mostly at Throcking in Hertfordshire, in the home of William Hyde, a member of the Dudley affinity. His house was conveniently placed between Norfolk and the capital. Amy and Robert also sometimes stayed with Amy's relatives on her mother's side, the Scotts of Camberwell near London who also owned a house in Kent, Hay's Court.[4]

In August 1557, Robert and his brothers went to the wars. King Philip was fighting the French in their own country, a campaign that culminated in the battle and siege of St. Quentin, near Paris. Robert and his brothers were allowed – and probably expected – to raise contingents on their own expenses. Robert left in early August, and his wife was now in charge of affairs:

---

1 Loades 1989 pp. 270–271, 360
2 Adams 2002 p. 158
3 Machyn p. 128
4 Adams 2008b

Mr. Flowerdew, I understand by Gryse that you put him in remembrance of that you spoke to me of, concerning the going of certain sheep at Syderstone; and although I forgot to move my lord thereof before his departing, he being sore troubled with weighty affairs and I not being altogether in quiet for his sudden departing, yet, notwithstanding, knowing your accustomed friendship towards my lord and me, I neither may nor can deny you that request, in my lord's absence, of mine own authority. Yea, and [if] it were a greater matter, as if any good occasion may serve you to try me; desiring you further that you will make sale of the wool so soon as is possible, although you sell it for 6s. the stone, or as you would sell for yourself, for my lord so justly required me, at his departing, to see those poor men satisfied, as though it had been a matter depending on life. Wherefore I [hesitate] not to sustain a little loss thereby to satisfy my lord's desire, and so to send that money to Gryse's house to London, by Bridewell, to whom my lord hath given order for the payment thereof. And thus I end, always troubling you, wishing that occasion may serve to requite you. Until that time I must pay you with thanks. And so to God I leave you.

From Mr. Hyde's this 7 August
Your assured during life,
Amy Dudley[1]

Amy wants Mr. Flowerdew, her Norfolk neighbour and kinsman who now served as her steward, to sell "certain

---

1   Wilson 1981 pp. 94–95; Adlard 1870 pp. 21–22

sheep" in order to pay off some "poor men" in a business her husband could not complete due to his "sudden departing". Her words have been thoroughly analyzed, especially since the letter was formerly believed to have been written two years later, after Elizabeth I's succession.[1] Thus especially one phrase, "I not being altogether in quiet for his sudden departing", has gained a connotation of romantic distress – which it may keep with the new dating as well: She could not be certain to see her husband return from the wars; her youngest brother-in-law, Henry Dudley, was killed. On 3 September 1557 every church in London rang the bells "for the winning of Saint Quentin; and there was slain my lord Harry Dudley the younger son of the duke of Northumberland that was beheaded with many more at the winning of it."[2] Lord Harry had been killed during the storming on 27 August, by a cannonball. Robert saw it happen "before his own eyes".[3]

Amy's writing style is remarkably clear and elegant, yet her personality still shines through. A devoted and loving wife,[4] she nevertheless displays a sense of irony regarding Robert's fussing about the business "as though it had been a matter depending on life".

It is sometimes implied that Robert and Amy must have been estranged because they had no children. A surprisingly high number of 16th century marriages remained childless, though, among them very happy ones like that of Amy's sister-in-law Katherine Hastings and the last one of her brother-in-law Ambrose, Earl of Warwick. William Cecil, who was very critical, noted gleefully about Robert Dudley:

---

1 Adams 1995 p. 381
2 Machyn p. 150
3 Adams 2008b
4 Skidmore 2010 pp. 52–53 interprets her use of "my lord" as submissive. However, to speak of the husband as "my lord" was the standard formula for wives, and even Juliet does so after she is married (Shakespeare, *Romeo and Juliet*, III, 2).

Nuptiae steriles.
No brother had children and yet their wives have.
Himself married and no children.[1]

It is also possible, of course, that Amy suffered miscarriages, but it seems unlikely that she carried any children to full term who later died. As an English wife of the 16th century, Amy in theory was almost her husband's property.[2] Reality was slightly different, and although Amy's possessions were officially controlled by him, Robert apparently allowed her her own income from her inheritance.[3] She even had a say in land dealings. Robert had assigned part of the manor of Hales Owen, a property he had inherited from his mother, to Amy's jointure, and in spring 1558 the couple came to London to sell it. They jointly testified the deed by their signatures on 27 March at Christchurch.[4]

*

In early 1558, parliament finally lifted the attainder against Robert Dudley and all his siblings. They were now officially restored in blood, although they had to renounce any claims to their executed father's possessions.[5] Amy and Robert were now looking for a new residence of their own, a house in the country. By the summer of 1558 Robert believed to have found the ideal place, provided the rent was right. Mr. Flowerdew's services were again called upon. With Amy's

---

1 Wilson 1981 p. 188. Cecil was not quite correct, it was in his interest to ignore a short-lived daughter Ambrose Dudley had had with his first wife (Adams 2008a).
2 Fraser 1996 p. 27; Skidmore 2010 p. 52
3 Adams 1995 p. 383
4 Adams 1995 p. 381; Skidmore 2010 p. 58; Adams 2002 p. 160. Jointure was land the wife was entitled to keep after her husband's death.
5 Adams 2008b

brother-in-law James Bigot, the husband of her half-sister Anne Appleyard, Flowerdew inspected the envisaged hall at Flitcham, near Syderstone. He was also to take care of everything else, for – true to his class – Lord Robert could or would not do what he should have done himself:

> Good Mr. Flowerdew, I do most heartily thank you for your pains and travail you have taken for me, as well touching the matter of Flitcham, as other mine affairs at Sidesterne. For the first, I would very gladly proceed therein, having it so as to be no loser by such rates as might be too over high set. For that, as I said before, I shall refer unto you, in thinking the prices too unreasonable, I must, if to dwell in that country, take some house other than mine own, for it there wanteth all such chief commodities as a house requireth, which is, pasture, wood, water, etc. To this I understand there is most of that the other wants, and besides it standeth somewhat nigh that little I have there. And where your care is so great for me in looking for my commodity herein, that you would have more advice than your own, for your contentation (though both your skill will suffice for a much greater matter than this, and my trust would not refuse that you should do in a greater matter also), I have required my brother Bige [Bigot] to take pains with you, and what order you take as well for the rent and prices, as for the year, I will accept and agree unto. Praying you that if you conclude that I may have a full certificate that the ground is what the stock is upon it already and what number of cattle you judge it may keep. And hearing hereof from you both, God willing, I will immediately come down

to see it myself, and to take further order by your advices for my coming thither.

I understand also that there is stuff or furniture in the house, which the executors will depart with all; I pray you I may have some little inventory what it is, and how they will leave it, and I will send word again what I will do. If it be good and worth the prices, I would not refuse it. For Sidestern, first for the fold-course [sheep-pens] at Boxford, I do mind to store and lay it myself, praying you to give your order for it; and for all things else that is out of order, I pray you to redress it at your discretion, as well [as] for placing or displacing such servants or shepherds as be unmeet to have charge there, even in such sort as any way I would or should do myself. And think myself much beholding and greatly in your debt, for the friendship you have divers ways showed me. And so with my hearty commendations, and ready to do you all the pleasure I may, I bid you farewell.

From Hays, this Friday morning.
Yours assured,
R. Duddeley[1]

This letter was written from Hay's Court, Kent, a house of Amy Dudley's maternal relations. Yet whatever Flowerdew's report, nothing came of the new home before England had a new queen and little remained as it was for Amy and Robert.

---

1 Adlard 1870 pp. 16–17

TWO

A FAVOURITE'S WIFE

On 10 November 1558 the Lady Elizabeth dined with the Spanish Count of Feria, Philip II's ambassador extraordinary, and the impression the count gained from this encounter let him to believe that among those "with whom she is on very good terms" was "Milord Robert".[1] Robert was very likely to fill an important position at the new court. On the morning after Elizabeth's accession, on 18 November, he was at Hatfield witnessing the ceremonial surrender of the Great Seal of England to the new queen. He became Master of the Horse later in the day. William Cecil, now the queen's Principal Secretary, made a last minute attempt to stop this promotion when he suggested that Robert be sent to Spain as special ambassador to announce Elizabeth's accession to King Philip.[2]

One of the principal officers of the royal household, the Master of the Horse was "*the* personal body servant of the monarch" outside of the palace.[3] Thus, through his office Robert Dudley was "the only man in England officially allowed to touch the Queen."[4] An excellent horseman, he was also to show great professional interest in royal transport and accommodation, horse breeding, and the supply of horses for all occasions. Amy's husband was thus perfectly suited to his

---
1 Rodríguez-Salgado and Adams 1984 pp. 322, 332
2 Adams 2008b
3 Murphy 2012
4 Whitelock 2013 p. 34

new job. Soon, Robert was asked to contact his former math teacher, the magus John Dee, so that the latter could choose the optimal date for the coronation. This was set for 15 January 1559, and Robert was entrusted with organizing and overseeing a large part of the festivities in the City of London.[1] He must have been extremely busy.

Amy Dudley, on the other hand, was no part in all this. She still resided at Throcking, Hertfordshire, and spent the Christmas season in Lincolnshire.[2] What connections exactly she had there we do not know, but it is likely she visited relatives. Robert came to Throcking around 1 April 1559, during the Easter recess of parliament, in which he sat as a member for Norfolk.[3] He stayed only a few days, playing cards with Mr. Hyde. He lost all the time, as his bookkeeper noted under "Pleying monnye":

> To Mr. Hide which he lent your Lordship at pley at his owne house} xls.
> Item deliveryd to your lordship at Mr Hides at sundry times viz by my hands xxs., by Hugans xixs., and by Mr Aldersham xxviiis.} lxvijs.[4]

*

Robert was back at court when on 18 April the Spanish ambassador, Count de Feria, reported startling news:

> Lord Robert has come so much into favour that he does whatever he likes with affairs and it is even said that her majesty visits him in his chamber day and night. People talk of this so

---

1 Wilson 1981 pp. 78, 83–92
2 Adams 1995 p. 377
3 Virgoe 1982
4 Adams 1995 p. 99. That was a total of 107s or £5 7s.

freely that they go so far as to say that his wife has a malady in one of her breasts and the Queen is only waiting for her to die to marry Lord Robert.[1]

From the Spanish original it appears that her condition was said to be even more serious, for *"está muy mala de un pecho"*[2] translates literally to "she is *very ill* in one breast", not just that she was suffering from "a malady" in it. About a fortnight later these news had arrived in Brussels at King Philip's court, Paolo Tiepolo, the Venetian ambassador, informing the Doge and Senate on 4 May 1559. He put all the interesting stuff in cipher:

> Lord Robert Dudley, Master of the Horse, and son of the late Duke of Northumberland, *a very handsome young man, towards whom in various ways the Queen evinces such affection and inclination that many persons believe that if his wife, who has been ailing for some time, were perchance to die, the Queen might easily take him for her husband.*[3]

Interestingly, the Venetian ambassador in London, Il Schifanoya, on 10 May, knew nothing of Amy Dudley's ill-health, although he too imparted "the opinion of many" about Lord Robert's intimacy with the queen; however, since he did not write in cipher he did not say everything: "it is better to keep silence than to speak ill".[4]

Tiepolo at Brussels, for his part, may even have been drawing on de Feria's report, which would have just arrived

---

1 CSP Simancas I pp. 57–58
2 Adams 1995 p. 63
3 CSP Ven 4 May 1559. Italics in cipher.
4 CSP Ven 10 May 1559

there when he wrote home to Venice. However this may be, the Count de Feria's version should not be easily dismissed. The count was one of Philip's most trusted confidants and known for his frankness.[1] He deeply mistrusted and disliked Queen Elizabeth, but he was acutely aware of her feelings. There could be no question that she was in love with her Master of the Horse. De Feria concluded that it was wise to cultivate him: "I can assure your Majesty that matters have reached such a pass that I have been brought to consider whether it would not be well to approach Lord Robert on your Majesty's behalf, promising him your help and favour, and coming to terms with him."[2]

Count de Feria had recently married Jane Dormer, a first cousin of Sir Henry Sidney, Robert Dudley's brother-in-law. Sidney was in Ireland during these months, but his wife, Mary, was in England and one of Elizabeth's closest ladies. She was also close to her brother Robert. Thus, in early 1559 de Feria may well have had access to information from inside the Dudley family circle.

*

A few weeks into her reign, Elizabeth had granted Robert Dudley a large house at Kew. This was a useful residence for someone who moved increasingly among princes. Robert, and as we shall see, Amy, still sometimes used Christchurch in London, now in possession of the Duke of Norfolk, who had married young Henry Dudley's widow. In a similar way, Robert's house at Kew was also used by his sister, Mary Sidney.[3]

We do not know whether Amy stayed in the house at Kew, though, when she travelled to London in May 1559. Her

---
1 Loades 2008
2 CSP Simancas I p. 58
3 Adams 1995 p. 142

health had improved. This is confirmed by the recently arrived new Spanish ambassador, Bishop Álvaro de la Quadra. He wrote on 6 June that "the wife of Milord Robert is already much better", and that she was taking great care about what she ate on the advice of the doctors.[1]

The reason for Amy's visit was probably that her husband was now a Knight of the Garter. The ceremony in April 1559 had caused "great wonder", and the other new knights had been Thomas Howard, 4th Duke of Norfolk, England's only duke, the Marques of Northampton, and the Earl of Rutland.[2] Now the wife of one of the most prominent people in the country,[3] Amy hired no less than twelve horses for her trip to the capital, which cost her husband 60 shillings.[4]

She stayed in London for about a month; her visit ended when Robert moved to Greenwich with the entire court. We cannot be entirely certain that Amy even saw Robert during her stay, although it seems likely enough. What does seem certain, however, is that she did not appear at court. She stayed in her mother's family home, Camberwell, and at Christchurch. With Robert in Greenwich with the queen, Amy continued her journey to Suffolk. It is unknown why and when exactly she stayed there.[5] She did receive 11 pistols (a Spanish gold coin) into her purse however, or £23 13s 4d.[6] She had only received £10 for her trip to London, so perhaps she had shopped more than anticipated.

Robert Dudley, meanwhile, was busy acting as host at state occasions and banquets with foreign ambassadors and

---

1 Adams 1995 p. 68; Lettenhove I p. 536 ("Su muger de milort Robert esta ya buena, y dicen que muy sobre el aviso en no comer cosa que no sea con mucha salva.")
2 CSP Simancas I p. 68; Wilson 1981 p. 96
3 The Spanish ambassador judged Robert Dudley to be one of three persons who "rule everything", the others being William Cecil and his brother-in-law Nicholas Bacon (CSP Simancas I p. 68).
4 Jackson 1878 p. 85
5 Adams 1995 p. 382–383
6 Jackson 1878 p. 85

princes.[1] By the autumn of 1559, several European princes were interested in the queen's hand; the best prospects had the emperor's son, Archduke Charles of Austria, and the Swedish crown prince, Eric. The latter sent his brother, John, to England, to woo in his place. He was welcomed at Colchester by the Earl of Oxford and Lord Robert who escorted him to London.[2] On 16 October, Robert gave "a grett bankett" for the "Prince of Sweden".[3]

The Habsburg ambassadors, meanwhile, got impatient. They had come to the conclusion that Elizabeth was fooling them, being only interested in Lord Robert. Earlier in the year, de Feria had already noticed that Elizabeth never let her favourite leave her side.[4] Wild assumptions were made about the queen's plans. "Lord Robert", the new Spanish ambassador de Quadra was convinced, was the man "in whom it is easy to recognise the king that is to be … she will marry none but the favoured Robert."[5]

There were now even rumours of sinister goings-on regarding Lady Amy Dudley. On 12 November 1559, the German nobleman and Imperial ambassador, Caspar von Breuner, wrote of a conspiracy between Elizabeth and Lord Robert to keep foreign suitors "in dalliance with mere words" until the couple were free to marry: "It is said that he seeks to poison his wife, for he is indeed a great favourite with the Queen".[6] The next day, 13 November, his fellow lodger, de Quadra, wrote the same. Philip's ambassador had heard from a "certain person who is accustomed to give me veracious news that Lord Robert has sent to poison his wife":

> Certainly all the Queen has done with us and with

---

1 HMC Bath V p. 9
2 Adams 1995 p. 100
3 Machyn p. 215
4 CSP Simancas I p. 63
5 Chamberlin 1939 p. 118
6 von Klarwill 1928 p. 152

the Swede, and will do with the rest in the matter of her marriage, is only keeping Lord Robert's enemies and the country engaged with words until this wicked deed of killing his wife is consummated. The same person told me some extraordinary things about this intimacy, which I would never have believed.[1]

Unfortunately, we have no idea who this person was who gave the ambassador such shocking news. It is even possible that it was his room mate Caspar von Breuner. Elizabeth was still not making any notable steps towards marrying the archduke and von Breuner was seriously angry with Robert:

> Although he is married to a beautiful wife he is not living with her, and, as I have been told by many persons, is trying to do away with her by poison. For this reason I think that the Queen and he have a secret understanding.[2]

Amy Dudley having apparently never visited the court, von Breuner probably never set eyes on her. Even his remarks about her being a "beautiful" woman have thus to be seen in context. He did not like Robert Dudley and tried to put him in a bad light. He saw in Robert the chief obstacle to the queen's marriage. If Elizabeth had indeed married the Archduke Charles this would have been very good for the ambassador's career. At the beginning of his stay in England, von Breuner had been confident that this would happen, although he had soon heard talk concerning Elizabeth's private life with Lord Robert that did not please him at all. He had then employed a spy to investigate among the queen's women. The result was that he heard about an incident where

---

1 CSP Simancas I p. 112
2 von Klarwill 1928 p. 157

Elizabeth herself had wondered "how any single person could be displeased, seeing that she was always surrounded by her ladies of the bedchamber and maids of honour, who at all times could see whether there was anything dishonourable between her and her Master of the Horse." – "This Master of the Horse", von Breuner had then explained, "is, I hear, married to a fine lady, from whom he has always had nothing but good. Nevertheless, since the Queen was crowned he has never been away from Court."[1] Such news was not able to disperse the emperor's suspicions and he became a good deal less keen to wed his son to the Queen of England. Elizabeth likewise lost interest towards the end of 1559.

Thus, after six months in England, the frustrated von Breuner had developed an astonishing hatred of Robert:

> I really do believe that he will follow in the footsteps of his parents [be executed like Robert's father and grandfather], and may the Devil be his companion, for he causes me and all who are active on behalf of his Princely Highness a world of trouble. He is so hated ... that it is a marvel that he has not been slain long ere this, for whenever they behold him they wish he might be hanged. ... I am certain he will one day meet with the reward he so richly merits. It is just like him to protract this marriage until he has sent his wife to Eternity.[2]

There was indeed a lot of dislike of the favourite now. Two of the highest-ranking noblemen in England, the Duke of Norfolk and the Earl of Arundel (the latter of whom was the father of the former's late wife), made no secret of it. Norfolk was overheard saying that Lord Robert would not die in his

---
1   von Klarwill 1928 pp. 114–115
2   von Klarwill 1928 p. 158

bed and that they would not "put up with his being King".[1] There may indeed have been several assassination plans; there were certainly plenty of rumours,[2] and Robert took to wearing a light, protective coat of mail under his clothes.[3]

Not too surprisingly, less than a year into the new queen's reign, there also appeared claims that Elizabeth was pregnant by Lord Robert, that he had "swived" her. A drunkard was arrested in Totnes as he told people these remarkable news.[4] Stories like this continued to be told for the rest of Elizabeth's life.[5]

*

Ever since the publication of Sir Walter Scott's novel *Kenilworth* in 1821, Robert Dudley has been criticized for effectively leaving his wife, hiding her away in the country, while dedicating himself to his court career. This criticism is of course entirely anachronistic and was even unrealistic throughout the 19th and 20th centuries. As we have seen from his finances, Robert could simply not have afforded the idle life of a country gentleman, sitting at home with his wife, in the longer term. It would also have been totally untypical for his class. He was a young man, and a younger son, and the court (where he had grown up) was his natural element. Quite apart from this, his family, not least his country-loving elder brother, expected him to make a career for the benefit of them all. The St. Quentin campaign had almost bankrupted Ambrose Dudley, so that he even had had to dismiss his music master and in August 1559 he asked his brother for a gift of hawks – "for I am so destitute".[6]

---

1 CSP Simancas I pp. 113–114
2 Adams 1995 p. 78; Wilson 1981 p. 100; Loades 2004 p. 269
3 Adams 1995 p. 151
4 Neale 1992 p. 83
5 Skidmore 2010 p. 141
6 HMC Bath V pp. 146, 166; Adams 2008a

Robert had originally supported the suit of the archduke for the queen's hand, which at first had also been supported by Philip II – and Robert Dudley had always been on good terms with the Spanish king, feeling an obligation to him for helping his family in the difficult years under Mary.[1] Robert only changed his position when Elizabeth grew cold of the Habsburg match in late 1559. The Habsburg ambassadors, as we have seen, had their own explanation for the queen's game – her love for Lord Robert.

It is interesting to compare the Habsburg dispatches with those of the French ambassador, who had no candidate in the race for Elizabeth's hand. Quite a lot of his correspondence for this time is still extant, however he writes nothing about poison for Robert's wife. Ambassador de Noailles had "very close social contact" with Lord Robert and yet he did not write much about him at all. It is possible that the Habsburg dispatches have been overrated.[2]

It is possible, though by no means certain, that after her visit to London in May–June 1559 Amy never saw her husband again.[3] He planned a visit to her a year later, in June 1560, making arrangements for an extended tour through the

---

1   Adams 2008b
2   Adams 1995 pp. 33–34: Robert Dudley's "contact with the Spanish embassy, as revealed in the accounts at any rate, was minimal. Therefore the comments on him in the Spanish despatches, which have been used extensively as sources, must be treated with some caution."
3   "Indeed, there is no evidence that they ever saw each other again after June 1559." (Adams 1995 p. 383). "It is also clear that after the summer of 1559 Dudley never saw his wife again." (Adams 2011). – This has become an often repeated fact. However, it is clear from an account book in the Dudley papers, Longleat, that Robert Dudley dined with Anthony Forster on the occasion of the christening of one of the latter's children, at some point between 20 December 1558 and 20 December 1559 (HMC Bath V p. 137). During this time Forster was living at Cumnor Place, Berkshire, the house Amy moved into sometime between September and December 1559. It is very likely that the christening would have taken place at Cumnor, but it is of course possible that Robert Dudley visited Forster before Amy moved into the latter's house. It is equally possible, though, that Robert visited his wife on the occasion.

Midlands, but the projected trip never materialized.[1] The queen's summer progress fell flat in 1560, thus depriving Robert of his chance to get away from the capital if not from court. His court office did not really allow him absences, and Queen Elizabeth did not really allow him a wife; according to contemporary court gossip he "was commanded to say that he did nothing with her, when he came to her, as seldom he did".[2]

The person who relayed this spicy detail was described as "P." and presumably wished to stay anonymous. Of course Elizabeth could not display, and perhaps did not feel, any hostility towards Amy, but she was no doubt emotionally affected by Amy's existence. As much later remarks to another Imperial ambassador by her make clear, she was keenly aware that Lord Robert was married.[3]

*

By September 1559, Amy Dudley was staying in the house of Sir Richard Verney, at Compton Verney in Warwickshire. Like Hyde, Verney, was an old member of the Dudley affinity, that is he was a gentleman who had served Robert Dudley's father, had enjoyed his patronage and was now seeking to continue this mutually beneficial relationship with his son.

Amy lived only for a few months (or weeks) in Verney's house, and by December 1559 had moved to Cumnor Place in what was then Berkshire, five miles from Abingdon and

---

[1] Adams 1995 pp. 141, 383; HMC Bath V pp. 157–158
[2] Adams, Archer, Bernard 2003b p. 66
[3] CSP Simancas I p. 437. "She then said, 'I have never said hitherto to anybody that I would not marry the earl of Leicester,' whereupon the envoy said she had told Preyner [von Breuner], who was formerly here on the same business, that she would not. 'But,' she replied, 'Lord Robert was married then, and there was no possibility of treating of such a thing at the time.'" (June 1565)

three miles from Oxford.[1] The house, the best on the spot, was owned by William Owen, son of Dr. George Owen, deceased court physician of Henry VIII. Dr. Owen had leased the place to Sir Anthony Forster, an arrangement continued by his son. Anthony Forster was a man of some standing in the counties of Berkshire and Oxfordshire;[2] a man of culture and a talented musician. He was above all a key member of the Dudley affinity, growing up in their service and later administering the Duke of Northumberland's principal estates in the Midlands. He was also prepared to take risks, being involved, under Mary, in the conspiracy of Sir Henry Dudley.[3] Later he had handled important business transactions for Robert Dudley, involving hundreds of pounds.[4]

Anthony Forster lived at Cumnor with his family, as well as with Mrs. Odingsells and the elderly Mrs. Owen, relations of the house's owner. Cumnor Place had once been a summer retreat of the Abbot of Abingdon and had been built in the 1330s. The house, which had been altered in the 15th century, consisted of four wings around a courtyard 52 feet wide and 72 feet long. The north wing faced Cumnor's main road, and St. Michael, the parish church, was directly next door. Beyond the south side there was a terrace garden, and a fish pond opening onto a deer park.[5]

Garden, pond, and park were all reminders of the house's monastic past and the monks' agreeable life there, though the terraces were a fashionable new addition. They pointed to the current residents' cultured lifestyle.

The house's main entrance, a gatehouse, was situated in the north range together with four ground-floor rooms, while

---
1 Adams 1995 pp. 382–382; Skidmore 2010 p. 169
2 Wilson 2005 p. 247
3 Harding 1981
4 Skidmore 2010 p. 59, Adams 1995 pp. 39, 66, 120, 125
5 Inman n.d.; Skidmore 2010 pp. 169–171

there was a chapel in the south wing. The west side of the house was almost taken up by a great hall with a beautifully ornamented timber roof, measuring 44x22 feet. At its south end there was a separate entrance to the complex, with stairs leading up to a large room, Amy Dudley's chamber. At the other end of the courtyard, on the east side, there were nine smaller rooms on two floors. The five upper floor rooms were only accessed through the north wing, whose upper floor consisted of a long gallery. It had been only recently added; it was 60 feet long and 15 feet wide and accessed by a staircase at the north-west corner of the house.[1] Such fashionable "long galleries" served as art galleries, could be used as dancing halls, and allowed people to stroll and exercise regardless of the weather.

The people in the house would most often have met in the hall, especially the servants would have taken their meals in there and another much frequented place would have been the gallery. It is unclear whether the chapel was still functioning and if Amy, or Forster, employed a private chaplain. Her room was the best chamber in the house. It was lit by a large window in the Late Gothic style and would have been well-heated in winter.[2]

Amy Dudley had her own little household of about ten servants at Cumnor, an appropriate number for the wife of one of the country's most prominent figures. She received the proceeds of the Robsart estate (her parents' inheritance) directly into her hands, out of which money she seems to have paid her servants.[3]

Among those was her maid, Mrs. Picto, who gave important testimony after Amy's death; it shows how devoted she was to her mistress. The male servants Amy employed included one William Huggins or Huggenes, who frequently

---
1 Skidmore 2010 pp. 170–171
2 Skidmore 2010 p. 171
3 Adams 1995 p. 383; Adams 2011

ran errands for her, as well as three others "that wayteth upon my lady" and wore Robert Dudley's livery.[1] And there was also "my ladies boye".[2]

Amy would have passed some of her time with needlework, playing games, and reading. Some of these things she would have done in the company of other people living in the house. Sir Anthony Forster had a wife and young children, and Robert Dudley played godfather to one of them during 1559, dining with "Mr. Forster" on the occasion.[3]

Two other ladies resided at Cumnor Place, the owner's mother, Mrs. Anne Owen, and Mrs. Elizabeth Odingsells, a 41-year-old widow, who was related to the Owens by marriage. Like Amy with her own little entourage, these two ladies would have employed their own servants each, although less in number. As the wife of Lord Robert – the son of a duke (however disgraced) and the queen's great favourite who socialized with visiting foreign princes – Amy was the person of the highest rank in the small world of Cumnor. She was a lady. A lady capable of lording (or ladying) over other inhabitants of the house; on one Sunday she famously insisted on having much of the house to herself:

> she would not that day suffer one of her own sort to tarry at home, and was so earnest to have them gone to the fair, that with any of her own sort that made reason of tarrying at home she was very angry. And came to Mrs. Odingsells the widow ... who refused that day to go to the fair; and was very angry with her also. Because she said it was no day for gentlewomen to go in, but said the morrow was much better, and then she would go. Whereunto my Lady answered and said that she

---

1   Skidmore 2010 p. 172
2   Skidmore 2010 p. 147
3   HMC Bath V p. 137

might choose and go at her pleasure: but all hers should go, and was very angry. They asked who should keep her company if all they went. She said Mrs. Owen should keep her company at dinner.[1]

Although most members of the various households would presumably have taken their meals in the great hall, especially the servants, the ladies, it would seem, dined much more comfortably in their chambers.

From her maid Picto we know that Amy was a sincerely devout person who, at least towards the end of her life, prayed daily on her knees. She had grown up in, and married into, evangelical households and may have wished to attend services and sermons frequently. She may have used Cumnor Place's own private chapel, but next door was the Cumnor parish church of St. Michael's, and there she would have met other well-situated people. Apart from William Owen and Anthony Forster, who were the two wealthiest,[2] there were a handful of other men with whose wives Amy may have kept company. There were also a few wealthy widows and spinsters, for example, Dorothy Buckner and Elizabeth Mutlowe. Dorothy's lodgings were rich in carpets and cushions, and she was the proud owner of several gold rings.[3]

Amy may, of course, have also received visitors from further away than Cumnor and possibly would have made visits herself to friends residing in the surrounding countryside. There was, for example, the Norris family,[4] Henry Norris being the son of one of Anne Boleyn's unfortunate "lovers". He and his wife Margaret were to play an important part in the inquiries after Amy's death and in her

---

1   Skidmore 2010 pp. 381–382
2   Skidmore 2010 p. 210
3   Skidmore 2010 pp. 172–173
4   Wilson 1981 p. 118

funeral. It is unlikely, however, that Amy embarked on more extensive travels while staying at Cumnor, for this would probably have left some traces in her husband's account books. Wherever Amy and Robert stayed, being nearly always apart, messengers were sent back and forth between them with letters, money, and other things like food or clothes. None of the letters between husband and wife have survived, nearly all of the Dudley family's private correspondence having been lost. This circumstance has contributed to the erroneous notion that Amy led an abandoned, lonely existence, that she was hidden away. Among the servants Robert sent to his wife were one Gower, one Langham, one John Forrest, and one "John Jones and his fellows", while Huggins was "her man".[1] Among the items that featured in Robert Dudley's account books were:

> For a trunk saddle with ye appurtenances for carrying of my lady's apparel 20s
>
> To Thomas Jones to buy a hood for my lady 35s
>
> To Gilbert ye goldsmith for 6 dozen gold buttons of ye Spanish pattern, and for a little chain delivered to Mr. Forrest for my lady's use £30
>
> Two ells of fine Holland for to make my lady ruffs 12s
>
> To Smyth the mercer for 6 yards of velvet at 43s a yard: and 4 yards to the Spanish tailor for your Lordship's doublet: and 2 yards for guarding my lady's cloak 112s 6d

---

1   Jackson 1878 pp. 84–85

11 pistols [a Spanish coin] delivered to Huggins to put into her Ladyship's purse £26 13s 4d[1]

Thomas Blount, his own steward, was another man who apparently travelled frequently between Robert and his wife. We hear of "Mr. Blunt's horse-hire when he rode to my lady in the Christmas" of 1559, but we also hear of "blue sewing silk sent to my lady by Mr. Forster", together with a looking glass.[2] In June 1560 Robert sent "a velvet hat embroidered with gold for my lady", worth £3 6s 8d, and a supply of 10 pairs of velvet shoes, worth £3[3] (this particular kind of footwear needing frequent replacement).

Amy also ordered dresses and finery herself, from her London tailor, William Edney. She needed a lot of stuff, things like "freeze and buckram for the ruffs and collars" and "silk to set on the lace".

> [A] round kirtle of russet wrought velvet with a fringe ...
>
> a loose gown of damask, laced all thick over the guard ...
>
> a cloth and an apron ...; thin lace with pearls on each side [of] the edge ...; silk to set it on ...; pointing ribbon to the same ...; lace to the top of the apron ...; sarcenet to face it ...
>
> a petticoat of scarlet, with a broad guard of velvet, stitched with eight stitches ...
>
> a Spanish gown of russet damask ...

---

1 Jackson 1878 p. 85. "Mr. Forrest" is Anthony Forster.
2 Jackson 1878 p. 85; Adams 1995 p. 106
3 Skidmore 2010 p. 194

a round kirtle of black velvet, cut all over and fringed ...

a round kirtle, the forepart of velvet with a fringe of black silk and gold ...

a Spanish gown of velvet, with a fringe of black silk and gold[1]

To her tailor, Amy also addressed the second of her two surviving letters. It was written on 24 August 1560 and found in 1865 still *in situ,* pinned to Edney's bill addressed "to my Lorde Robarte Dudles wyffe" which he had sent to Robert after Amy's death. She wanted Edney to add a collar to a velvet gown she had recently purchased from him. The work should be done as quickly as possible and then sent back with the Oxford carrier, a man called Frewen:

> edney w[ith] my harty comendations these shalbe to desier you to take ye paynes for me As to make this gowne of vellet whiche I sende you w[ith] suche A collare as you made my rosset taffyta gowne you sente me last & I will se you dyscharged for all I pray you let it be done w[ith] as muche speade as you can & sente by this bearar frewen the carryar of oxforde / & &
> thus I bed you most hartely fare well from comnare this xxiiij of avguste
>
> Your assured frind
> Amye Duddley[2]

---

1 Jackson 1878 pp. 86–88
2 Jackson 1878 p. 66

THREE

MY WIFE IS DEAD

On Saturday, 7 September 1560, Robert Dudley, returning from a day out with the queen, wrote a letter to the Earl of Sussex in Ireland. He wrote that Elizabeth "thanks be to God is in very good health and is now become a great huntress and doth follow it daily from morning till night." He informed the earl that the queen intended to send for "some hobbies" from Ireland, some "strong good gallopers, which are much better than her geldings, whom she spareth not to tire as fast as they can go". Though he admitted that he feared those geldings "much", Robert wished that Elizabeth "may light up a good horse", for "surely she shall have a great good treasure & I shall think myself happy."[1]

On Monday, 9 September, Robert Dudley wrote another letter from Windsor Castle, this time to his steward and cousin, Sir Thomas Blount. Blount, as it happened, was on his way to Cumnor:

> Immediately upon your departing from me there came to me Bowes, by whom I do understand that my wife is dead, and as he saith by a fall from a pair of stairs. Little other understanding can I have of him. The greatness and the suddenness of the misfortune doth so perplex me, until I do hear from you how the matter standeth,

---

1 Adams 2002 pp. 135–136; Skidmore 2010 p. 197

or how this evil should light upon me, considering what the malicious world will bruit, as I can take no rest.

And, because I have no way to purge myself of the malicious talk that I know the wicked world will use, but one, which is the very plain truth to be known: I do pray you, as you have loved me and do tender me and my quietness. And as now my special trust is in you, that [you] will use all the devices and means you can possible for the learning of the truth; wherein have no respect to any living person.

And, as by your own travail and diligence, so likewise by order of law, I mean by calling of the coroner, and charging him to the uttermost from me to have good regard to make choice of no light or slight persons: But the discreetest and [most] substantial men for the Juries such as for their knowledge may be able to search thoroughly & duly by all manner of examinations the bottom of the matter: and for their uprightness will earnestly and sincerely deal therein without respect. And that the body be viewed and searched accordingly by them; and in every respect to proceed by order and law. In the mean time Cousin Blount let me be advertised from you by this bearer with all speed how the matter doth stand: For as the cause and the manner thereof doth marvellously trouble me, considering my case many ways, so shall I not be at rest till I may be ascertained thereof, praying you even as my trust is in you, and as I have ever loved you, do not dissemble with me, neither let anything be hid from me. But send me your true conceit and opinion of the matter, whether it happened by evil chance or by villainy. And fail not to let me hear continually from you. And thus fare you well in much haste from Windsor this ixth of September [in] the evening.

Your loving friend & kinsman
much perplexed
R. D.

I have sent for my brother Appleyard
because he is her brother and other of
her friends also to be there that they
may be privy and see how all things
do proceed.[1]

Robert's reaction to the news of his wife's death clearly shows his bewilderment, he has nevertheless often been criticized for immediately thinking "how this evil should light upon me". The set of five letters between him and Thomas Blount, written between 9 and 13 September 1560, survive only as copies and it was likely Robert himself who commissioned them. In 1567 there was an investigation by the privy council into Amy's case, and he may have wished to present copies of the letters.[2] It was not at all uncommon to make these, while keeping the originals. Much of Robert Dudley's archive was later destroyed, some of it as late as 1879,[3] and historians have never seriously suspected that the letters were tampered with. It is worth remembering that without them we would know very little indeed about Amy Dudley.

---
1   Skidmore 2010 pp. 379–380; Pettigrew 1859 p. 28
2   Adams 2011
3   Adams 1995 pp. 4–5

When Thomas Blount arrived at Cumnor, the coroner's inquest had already started. Blount promised to report everything to his master and on the way he had already begun investigating:

> [T]oo true it is that my Lady is dead, and as it seemeth with a fall; but yet how or which way I cannot learn. ... The same night I came from Windsor I lay at Abingdon all that night, and because I was desirous to hear what news went abroad in the country, at my supper I called for mine host, and asked him what news was there about, taking upon me I was going into Gloucestershire. He said, there was fallen a great misfortune within three or four miles of the town; he said my Lord Robert Dudley's wife was dead, and I asked him what was his judgement, and the judgement of the people; he said some were disposed to say well and some evil. What is your judgment said I: By my troth said he, I judge it a misfortune, because it chanced in that honest gentleman's house, his great honesty, said he, doth much curb the evil thoughts of the people.
>
> Methinks, said I, that some of her people that waited upon her should somewhat say to this. No sir, said he, but little; for it was said that they were all here at the fair, and none left with her. How might that chance, said I. Then said he it is said here, that she rose that day very early, and commanded all her sort to go [to] the fair and would suffer none to tarry at home; and thereof is much judged.
>
> And truly my Lord I did first learn of Bowes as I

met with him coming towards your lordship of his own ... that day; and of all the rest ... who affirmed that she would not that day suffer one of her own sort to tarry at home, and was so earnest to have them gone to the fair, that with any of her own sort that made reason of tarrying at home, she was very angry; and came to Mrs. Odingsells the widow, that lieth with Anthony Forster, who refused that day to go to the fair; and was very angry with her also.

Because she [Mrs. Odingsells] said it was no day for gentlewomen to go in, but said the morrow was much better, and then she would go. Whereunto my Lady answered and said that she might choose, and go at her pleasure; but all hers should go, and was very angry. They asked who should keep her company if all they went; she said Mrs. Owen should keep her company at dinner. The same tale doth Picto, who doth dearly love her, confirm.

Certainly, my Lord, as little while as I have been here, I have heard divers tales of her that maketh me to judge her to be a strange woman of mind. In asking of Picto what she might think of this matter, either chance or villainy, she said by her faith she doth judge very chance, and neither done by man nor by herself: For herself, she said, she was a good virtuous gentlewoman, and daily would pray upon her knees, and divers times she saith that she hath heard her pray to God to deliver her from desperation. Then, said I, she might have an evil toy in her mind. No, good Mr.

> Blount, said Picto, do not judge so of my words; if you should so gather, I am sorry I said so much.
>
> My Lord, it is most strange that this chance should fall upon you. It passeth the judgement of any man to say how it is; but truly the tales I do hear of her maketh me to think she had a strange mind in her; as I will tell you at my coming.[1]

Clearly, Blount had a suspicion that Amy might have killed herself, and that her behaviour had been rather strange lately, the details of which he was going to tell Robert in person. His letter still continued, however, with the proceedings of the inquest:

> But to the inquest you would have so very circumspectly chosen by the coroner for the understanding of the truth, your Lordship needeth not to doubt of their well choosing. Before my coming the inquest were chosen and part of them at the house [Cumnor Place]. If I be able to judge of men and of their ableness, I judge them and specially some of them, to be as wise and as able men to be chosen upon such a matter as any men, being but countrymen, as ever I saw; and as well able to answer to their doing before whosoever they shall be called.
>
> And for their true search without respect of person: I have done your message unto them. I have good hope they will conceal no fault if any be, for as they are wise, so are they as I hear part of them very enemies to Anthony Forster. God

---

1 Skidmore 2010 pp. 381–382; Pettigrew 1859 pp. 29–30

give them, with their wisdom, indifferency, and then be they well chosen men.

> More advertisement, at this time, I cannot give your Lordship, but as I can learn so will I advertise, wishing your Lordship to put away sorrow and rejoice, whatsoever fall out, of your own innocency, by the which in time doubt not but that malicious reports shall turn upon their backs ... Your Lordship hath done very well in sending for Mr. Appleyard.[1]

Thus reassured by Blount against the evil talk of his enemies, Robert had time to ponder all possibilities and on 12 September sent another impatient letter:

> Cousin Blount until I hear from you again how the matter falleth out in very truth I cannot be in quiet; and yet you do well satisfy me with the discreet jury you say are chosen already: unto whom I pray you say from me, that I require them, as ever as I shall think good of them, that they will, according to their duties, earnestly, carefully, and truly deal in this matter, to find it as they shall see it fall out; and, if it fall out a chance or misfortune, then so to say; and if it appear a villainy (as God forbid so mischievous or wicked body should live), then to find it so. And God willing I shall never fear the dire prosecution accordingly, what person soever it may appear any way to touch; as well for the just punishment of the act as for mine own true justification, for as I would [be] sorry in my heart

---

1   Skidmore 2010 p. 382; Pettigrew 1859 p. 30

any such evil should be committed, so shall it well appear to the world my innocency by my dealing in the matter, if it shall so fall out.

And therefore, Cousin Blount, I seek chiefly truth in this case, which I pray you still to have regard unto without any favour to be showed either one way or other when you have done my message to them.

Robert was referring to the message to the coroner in his first letter three days earlier that "no light or slight persons" should be chosen, but only "the discreetest and [most] substantial men" who then should examine the case to the bottom of the matter". However, this was not enough and Blount should continue with his own inquiries:

> I require you not [sic] to stay to search thoroughly yourself always that I may be satisfied, and that with such convenient speed as you may.[1]

Thomas Blount, having been Robert's confidant for years (he had "bought" Hales Owen from Robert and Amy in 1558 for £3,000, only to sell it to a real customer for £2,000 a few month later[2]) was able to reassure his master the very next day. He told him that circumstances had convinced him that nothing suspicious had occurred; still, he could not but think it was strange that such a thing, whatever it was, had happened to Robert's wife.

> I have done your Lordship's message unto the jury, you need not to bid them to be careful:

---

1 Skidmore 2010 p. 383; Pettigrew 1859 p. 32
2 Adams 2002 p. 160

whether equity of the cause or malice to Forster do forbid it, I know not, they take great pains to learn the truth. To-morrow I will wait upon your Lordship and as I come I will break my fast at Abingdon, and there I shall meet with one or two of the jury; and what I can I will bring.

They be very secret; and yet do I hear a whispering that they can find no presumptions of evil. And if I may say to your Lordship my conscience: I think some of them be sorry for it, God forgive me. And if I judge amiss [sic], mine own opinion is much quieted, the more I search of it, the more free it doth appear to me.

I have almost nothing that can make me so much [as] to think that any man should be the doer thereof, as when I think your Lordship's wife before all other women should have such a chance. The circumstances and as many things as I can learn doth persuade me that only misfortune hath done it and nothing else.

Myself will wait upon your Lordship to-morrow, and say what I know; in the meantime I humbly take my leave, from Cumnor the xiiith September

Your L life & living
T.B.[1]

Meanwhile, Robert Dudley had received an interesting message:

---

1 Skidmore 2010 p. 384; Pettigrew 1859 pp. 30–31. The final formula is to mean "Your Lordship's while I live".

I have received a letter from one Smith, one that seemeth to be foreman of the jury. I perceive by his letters that he and the rest have and do travail very diligently and circumspectly for the trial of that matter which they have charge of, and for anything that he or they by any search or examination can make in the world hitherto, it doth plainly appear, he saith, a very misfortune, which for mine own part Cousin Blount doth much satisfy and quiet me.

Nevertheless, because of my thorough quietness and all others' hereafter, my desire is that they may continue in their inquiry and examination to the uttermost as long as they lawfully may; yea, and when these have given their verdict, though it be never so plainly found, assuredly I do wish that another substantial company of honest men might try again for the more knowledge of truth.

That the jury's foreman, Smith, wrote to Robert Dudley has been pointed out as an indication that Blount and Dudley perhaps pressurized the jury.[1] One may ask, though, what harm should have come from Robert reading Mr. Smith's letter, especially as he seems not to have known the man. The harbinger of welcome news, Mr. Smith without doubt wanted to make sure he acquired a thankful patron (and he may well have succeeded). What certainly appears from Robert's letter is that, while he was relieved to know that it was found "a very misfortune", he nevertheless thought that further investigation could do no harm. To this end he had sent Sir Richard Blount, "who is a perfect honest gentleman", and Mr. Norris, "to help to the furtherance thereof." Mr. Norris

---

1   Doran 1996 p. 228; Bernard 2000 pp. 170–171

was most probably the queen's friend and possible acquaintance of Amy's, Henry Norris of Rycote.

[L]ikewise Appleyard, I hear, hath been there as I appointed & Arthur Robsart, her brothers. If any more of her friends had been to hand, I would also have caused them to have seen and been privy to all the dealing there. Well, cousin, God's will be done and I wish he had made me the poorest that creepeth on the ground, so this mischance had not happened to me.

But, good cousin, according to my trust have care above all things that there be plain, sincere, and direct dealing for the full trial of this matter: Touching Smith and the rest, I mean no way to deal with them; but let them proceed in the name of God accordingly, and I am right glad they be all strangers to me. Thus fare you well, in much haste.
From Windsor

Your loving friend and kinsman
R.D.[1]

*

The inquest called by the queen's coroner (the gentleman John Pudsey) was performed by 15 jurors. All were local gentlemen or yeomen of substance: They were listed as Richard Smythe, Humphrey Lewys, Thomas Moulder, Richard Knyghte, Thomas Spyre, Edward Stevenson, John Stevenson, Richard Hewse, William Cantrell, William Noble,

---

1 Skidmore 2010 pp. 384–385; Pettigrew 1859 p. 31

John Buck, John Kene, Henry Langley, Stephen Ruffyn, and John Syre.[1] These men assembled on 9 September 1560, the day after Amy's death, and reached a verdict in less than a week. The verdict's pronouncement, however, was "adjourned from the aforesaid ninth day onwards day by day very often" at the jurors' request, until they appeared again before the judges of assizes on 1 August 1561.[2] A sinister meaning has been read into these supposed delays,[3] however all this was the usual practice; the verdict was registered at the day of the assizes and then "lodged ... with the court of king's bench".[4] It was there that the coroner's report of the inquest was filed away under the year 1561, not 1560, which is why no historian has found it until 2008, when Dr. Steven Gunn of Oxford University rediscovered it by chance doing research for a study of accidental deaths in Tudor England.[5] The report, written in Latin, concludes that

> Lady Dudley ... being alone in a certain chamber ... and intending to descend the aforesaid chamber by way of certain steps (in English called 'steyres') of the aforesaid chamber there and then accidentally fell precipitously down the aforesaid steps to the very bottom of the same steps, through which the same Lady Amy there and then sustained not only two injuries at her head (in English called 'dyntes') – one of which was a quarter of a thumb deep and the other two thumbs deep – but truly also, by reason of the accidental injury or of that fall and of Lady Amy's own body weight falling down the

---

1 Skidmore 2010 pp. 210, 377; TNA KB 9/1073/f.80
2 TNA KB 9/1073/f.80
3 Skidmore 2010 p. 233
4 Adams 2011
5 *Elizabeth I: Killer Queen?*

aforesaid stairs, the same Lady Amy there and then broke her own neck, on account of which certain fracture of the neck the same Lady Amy then and there died instantly; and the aforesaid Lady Amy was found then and there without any other mark or wound on her body; and thus the jurors say on their oath that the aforesaid Lady Amy in the manner and form aforesaid by misfortune came to her death and not otherwise, as they are able to agree at present.[1]

Amy Dudley, stepping out of her room, had fallen down the adjoining stairs, breaking her neck. It had been an accident.

*

After Elizabeth had announced Amy's death she ordered mourning for more than a month, and the court became "stuffed with mourners", according to an eyewitness.[2]

> Thenterment of the right noble lady Amey Robsert, late wyffe to the right noble the lord Robert Dudelley, knight and compaignion of the moste noble ordre of the Garter and master of the horsse to the queenes moste excellent majestie

was to be held at Oxford:

> Fyrste, after that the said lady was thus departed out of this transsetory world, she was saffely

---

1 TNA KB 9/1073/f.80; Skidmore 2010 pp. 232, 377. The National Archives' translation has "inch"/"inches" for the Latin "pollex"/"pollices", which more precisely means "thumb". The inch, however, is believed to have originated from the width of a thumb (see below p. 66).
2 Wright I p. 45–46; Wilson 1981 p. 122

cered and coffened, and so remayned there tyll Fryday ... on the which day she was secreately brought to Glouster college a lytell without the towne of Oxford, the which plasse of Gloster couledge was hanged with blake cloth and garnesshed with skocheons [escutcheons] of his armes and heres in palle, that is to say, a great chamber where the morners did dyne, and at there chamber where the gentillwomen did dyne, and beneth the steres a great hall, all which places as afforesaid were hanged with blake cloth and garnesshed with skochions; the howsse beinge thus furnesshed ther the corsse remayned till the buryall, and till suche tyme as all things were redy for the same.[1]

On 22 September 1560, a fortnight after her death, Amy Dudley was laid to rest at the University Church of St. Mary the Virgin, the alma mater's oldest building and one of the city's most recognizable sites. Inside St. Mary's, an elaborately carved hearse had been constructed to receive Amy's coffin for the funeral. The church was likewise draped in black cloth and the hearse measured 7 ½ feet of width and 14 feet of height, "in the which tope of the hersse was set two skochions of armes on paste paper in metall wrought with compartements of gold".[2] Also a valance of black sarcenet was hung from the hearse, "written with letters of gold".[3]

The chief mourner was Lady Margery Norris, the queen's good friend and her "own dear crow". Six women of Cumnor featured at the ceremony, walking in pairs behind the chief mourner:

---

1 Adlard 1870 p. 52. "Cered" means embalmed.
2 Adlard 1870 p. 53
3 Skidmore 2010 p. 217

Mrs. Wayneman and my lady Pollard.
Mrs. Doylly and Mrs. Buteller thelder.
Mrs. Blunte and Mrs. Mutlowe,[1]

Elizabeth Mutlowe being one of Amy's neighbours.[2] Her half-brother, Sir John Appleyard, walked in front of the coffin, in a "long gown, his hood on his head". Also among the official mourners was the mayor of Oxford with "his brethren". The procession from Gloucester Hall to St. Mary's was lead by two "conductors" with black staves, followed by 80 poor persons, men and women, pairs of professors and doctors, and finally the choir.[3] Robert Dudley had also booked a detachment of royal heralds under Garter, Lancaster, and Clarenceux kings of arms, as well as Rouge Croix pursuivant. They were to oversee and write down everything, and were paid the sum of £56 16s 8d for their "paynes abought my ladies funerales at Oxfurth".[4] Robert also paid for a "parryes head", perhaps a hat made in Paris, and "other furnyture", probably clothing or accoutrements for the chief mourner.[5] The whole proceedings cost Amy's widower more than £2,000.[6] The London undertaker, Henry Machyn, was pleased to note:

> The [blank] day of August [sic] was bered my lade Dudley the wyff of my lord Robart Dudley the master of the quen['s] horse, with a grett baner of armes and a vj baners-rolles of armes, and a viij dosen penselles and viij dosen skochyons, and iiij grett skochyons of armes, and

---

1 Adlard 1870 p. 54
2 Skidmore 2010 pp. 173, 217
3 Skidmore 2010 pp. 216–217; Adlard 1870 p. 54
4 Adams 1995 p. 125; Wilson 1981 p. 123
5 Adams 1995 p. 132
6 Wright I p. 47

iiij haroldes, master Garter, master Clarenshux, master Lanckostur, and [blank].[1]

The funeral oration in St. Mary's was made by Dr. Francis Babington, Master of Balliol College, and "Doctor of Devynytie". He preached on the theme of "*Beati mortui qui in Domino moriuntur*", "Blessed are they who die in the Lord".[2] The scurrilous anti-Dudley libel, *Leicester's Commonwealth*, 24 years later claimed that he made a slip of the tongue, describing Amy as "this lady so pitifully slain". However, that Dr. Babington said anything like this is highly unlikely as he was "a celebrated trimmer" (in the words of Leicester's biographer Derek Wilson) who had not only pursued a successful career in the church of Henry VIII, Edward VI, Mary I, and Elizabeth I, but was now also a protégé of Robert Dudley.[3]

Robert Dudley was not there to hear any embarrassing remarks himself; it was customary for widowers to stay away from their wives' funeral. He wore mourning for half a year and paid Amy's outstanding bills. He also paid £25 6s 8d to redeem a diamond she had given in pawn to Richard Whetell, merchant of the Staple.[4]

---

1   Machyn p. 242
2   Adlard 1870 p. 55; Skidmore 2010 p. 217
3   Wilson 1981 p. 123. The Elizabethan Jesuit Robert Parsons claimed that his martyred colleague Edmund Campion had played a role in the event: "Edmund Campion was chosen, though then very young, to make an English oration in her funerals, which he performed with exceeding commendation of all who were present." (Simpson 1896 pp. 9–10). If true, it is unclear how this would have worked. It is clear that Campion, who was only 20 in 1560, was a *protégé* of Robert Dudley then or later, but it is unlikely that there were two funeral sermons in St. Mary's church. It is possible though that her death was commemorated also in some of the colleges. Campion was a student at St. John's College.
4   Adams 1995 p. 125

FOUR

ACCIDENT?

The coroner's jury found that Amy Dudley had fallen down the stairs and died from an accident. Many people at the time did not believe this and many modern commentators have likewise questioned that one could die from such a fall downstairs as Amy seemed to have suffered. Unfortunately, we do not really know a lot about those stairs. Robert Dudley mentioned that Bowes, the servant who brought him the news of his wife's death, had told him that she had died "by a fall from a paire of stayres" and Thomas Blount later confirmed that she was dead, "and as it seamethe with a fall".[1] The Spanish ambassador de Quadra likewise concluded, immediately after hearing from the queen that Amy had broken her neck, that "[s]he must have fallen down a staircase."[2]

The coroner's report was slightly more precise, detailing that Lady Amy had meant to "descend the aforesaid chamber by way of certain steps (in English called 'steyres') of the aforesaid chamber there and then accidentally fell precipitously down the aforesaid steps to the very bottom of the same steps".[3] The English jurors specified in their Latin report that "gradus" (steps) was "stairs" in English.

Cumnor Place was pulled down in 1811, but an early 19th century description survives of one of the staircases at

---
1   Skidmore 2010 pp. 381, 379
2   CSP Simancas I p. 176
3   TNA KB 9/1073/f.80

Cumnor Place, as does a drawing of the same time. The description speaks of a "circular newel stone staircase".[1] The drawing appears to show what could also be called a winder staircase within a quadrangular frame, with a small landing in one of the corners. At the landing the stairs turn by 180 degrees. It is unclear from the sketch, though, where the stairs begin and end, i.e. which part is the upper and which the lower one. The whole staircase appears to have about 12 or 13 steps, the landing included.[2]

It has been assumed that Amy was found at this staircase.[3] It led to the long gallery, however, whereas the coroner's report clearly speaks of stairs which led down from a "chamber" (*camera*) in which Lady Amy was alone. A room where she would have been alone would have been her separate chamber at the other end of the house in the south corner of the west wing – and there was also a staircase. The coroner's report would hardly have confused a chamber with a long gallery, a quite different architectural element. Nor would Amy likely have been alone in the gallery (we remember that she had only sent away her own servants, she could not have sent away the Forsters' servants or Mrs. Odingsells' or Mrs. Owen's).

It is possible that the staircase adjoining Amy's chamber was of a similar type than the staircase leading to the long gallery, but we cannot be sure. The only thing we know with certainty about it is that it led down to a separate entrance with a doorway.[4]

Importantly, people who had direct information from the scene of Amy's death did not mention anything much specific about the stairs. It is two highly problematic sources (in that

---

1 Skidmore 2010 p. 220
2 BL Additional MS 9460 f.74.b.; Skidmore 2010 p. 220; Inman n.d.
3 It is important to note that the staircase shown in the sketch may have been built after Amy Dudley's death, e.g. during building works in the 1570s (Inman n.d.).
4 Skidmore 2010 p. 171

they only report *talk* the writers heard in London and in that they are extremely hostile to Robert Dudley) which add further details about Amy's fall, or supposed fall. First, there is a so-called journal (written c.1561–1563[1]) that describes how "she was the cause of her own death, falling down a pair of stairs, which by report was but eight steps."[2] The writer, who is unknown but was clearly based in London, says that he did not know Robert Dudley and did not recognize him when he came to court: "And for my self I knewe him not, for I never sawe him before, ne knewe not yt was he tyll he was paste." – Clearly, he was not part of his circle and would not have had first hand knowledge of the circumstances of Amy's death.[3]

Then there is the satirical libel known as *Leicester's Commonwealth*, written c.1584, which claims that "shortly after" Robert had sent Amy to Oxford, "she had the chance to fall from a pair of stairs and so to break her neck, but yet without hurting of her hood that stood upon her head."[4]

Since the pamphlet was for several centuries the most important source for Robert Dudley's life story, this detail has been firmly entrenched in historical writing and to this day appears as a fact in countless books. We shall see that the rest of Amy's story as related by *Leicester's Commonwealth* is riddled with manifest errors, or rather, freely invented, so there is no good reason to believe this particular detail about her hood. It was clearly intended as a satirical remark and there is no other source dealing with her death that would mention any of her clothes.

*

---

[1] Adams, Archer, Bernard 2003b pp. 40–41
[2] Adams, Archer, Bernard 2003b p. 66
[3] Adams, Archer, Bernard 2003b p. 67
[4] Peck 1985 p. 58

The notion that Amy Dudley could not really have died from falling down the stairs is widespread, whether because it is felt that those stairs were somehow too short or because her hood supposedly remained undisturbed. More recently, the contents of the coroner's report have been added as a reason why she could not have died from a stair accident, although the report itself clearly states that she did.

Though the report must ultimately remain inconclusive – it is after all a piece of paper, not a skull or skeleton – the injuries it describes are compatible with an accident.[1] According to comparative forensic pathological studies it is not at all uncommon to die from falling down the stairs. In studies that tried to determine methods to distinguish between head injuries received from a fall and from blows, stair falls figured as a typical death cause.[2] The location, length, and number of lacerations were the most important parameters in comparative forensic studies.[3] Head injuries are the single most common injuries in stair falls generally, "comprising 36% of all injuries."[4] It is not unusual in falls downstairs that no other wounds on the trunk of the body are sustained, as occurred in Amy's case.[5] Injuries of the lower extremities are much more common, accounting for about 44% of injuries in adults.[6] Amy Dudley did not break her leg, of course, but it can also be questioned whether the jury would have recognized a sprained ankle, for example.

Unfortunately, the coroner's report gives no indication where the head injuries were located. If Amy sustained these wounds through a fall it is likely this occurred by hitting her

---

1 Adams 2011
2 Kremer et al. 2008; Kremer and Sauvageau 2009; Maxeiner and Ehrlich 2000; Ehrlich and Maxeiner 2002
3 Guyomarc'h et al. 2010; Maxeiner and Ehrlich 2000; Kremer et al. 2008
4 Skidmore 2010 p. 232; Templer 1992 p. 19. For juvenile victims under 20 this figure is even higher, about 58% (Templer 1992 p. 19).
5 Skidmore 2010 pp. 232–233
6 Templer 1992 p. 19 ("ages 20 and older").

head on the edges of stair treads. Edges of stair treads are by no means harmless, as they account for 50% of head injuries sustained in stair falls. On the other hand, Amy may also have suffered injuries from hitting some sharp object the way down.[1] It has been estimated that "handrails, balustrades, and adjoining walls" are responsible for 13% of injuries.[2] The author of a standard text on staircases concludes that "[a] fall downstairs is comparable to falling into a hole with jugged rocks at the bottom."[3]

Amy Dudley's wounds were described in the coroner's report as a quarter of a thumb and two thumbs deep, respectively. This translates to circa 0.5 cm (or 5 mm) and 5 cm, respectively.[4] A thumb corresponded to about an inch, and it is believed that the medieval origins of the inch as a unit stemmed from measuring the width of a thumb.[5]

To inspect Amy's injuries most likely a measuring rod would have been used, forcing it into the wounds with whatever influence on results. The first wound, "of the depth of a quarter of one thumb", would have constituted a flesh wound without damage to the skull bone. It might have looked very serious because of the high effusion of blood in head wounds, and it would have been gaping in case the lowest layer of the scalp (the *galea aponeurotica*) would have been cut through; this could just have happened at 5 mm depth, and the serious risk would have come from the danger of infection afterwards.[6] The second wound, "of the depth of two thumbs", would mean a skull fracture – either open ("compound") or closed ("depressed").[7]

---

1 Skidmore 2010 pp. 232, 233
2 Templer 1992 p. 23
3 Templer 1992 p. 23
4 Skidmore 2010 p. 232
5 Wikipedia: Inch
6 Frick, Leonhardt, Starck 1991 p. 663; Parsons 1929; Wikipedia: Scalp; Wikipedia: Kopfschwarte
7 Medscape: Imaging in Skull Fractures; Wikipedia: Skull fracture

Proponents of the murder theory like to point out that Amy was unlikely to suffer such injuries in falling down the stairs, especially if those stairs were not higher than eight steps. Nothing of this is untypical, however, and there always occur cases of serious and even fatal falls downstairs, as is borne out by statistical and forensic studies, but also by media reports. In Germany, in 2015 falls in general claimed the lives of 12,868 people, which is considerably more than the 10,080 suicides and 3,690 fatal road accidents.[1] Several thousand victims were over 75 years old, but there were still 343 people under 50 who died from a fall. Fatal stair falls amounted to 42 in the group under 50, with a total of 1,271 in all age groups, the group over 75 being again the largest with several hundred. In 826 of all fatal stair falls head injuries were the cause of death, that is almost two thirds. Neck injuries (which presumably includes broken necks) were responsible for 7.2% of deaths (92 cases).[2]

That both broken necks and skull fractures do occur in stair falls is apparent from media reports as well. For example in 2008 the single casualty of an earthquake in the Greek island of Rhodes was a 54-year-old woman who fell down the stairs in an attempt to leave her house. She slipped and broke her neck, the two-year-old grandchild on her arm survived unharmed.[3] In 2012 a German politician fell down the stairs in his house, sustaining multiple skull fractures (he survived due to intensive care).[4] In 2014 a Berlin schoolboy succumbed to his injuries after falling down the stairs during a day out with his class. The 12-year-old died on the spot.[5] Serious stair accidents will happen, and statistical studies

---

1 Statistisches Bundesamt 2017 p. 8
2 Statistisches Bundesamt 2017 pp. 29, 35. This includes "falls from or on stairs", as well as "falls from or on steps".
3 "Woman killed in Rhodes earthquake"; "Erdbeben im Urlaubsparadies"; "Touristen-Insel Rhodos von Erdbeben getroffen: Eine Tote"
4 "Linken-Politiker André Brie schwer verunglückt"
5 "Junge (12) stirbt bei Schulausflug"

have even demonstrated that the most dangerous stairs are short ones with under ten steps.[1]

*

Although, as we have seen, Amy might have died from an unexpected and sudden fall downstairs, even a short one, there is a widespread notion that extraordinary circumstances, like an illness, were needed to explain her death. That she might have been suffering from breast cancer has gained particular credence. The theory was first formulated in 1956 by Ian Aird, professor of medicine. Aird suggested that Amy's broken neck might have been caused by cancerous deposits in the spine, a condition occurring in many breast cancer patients. This would have made the affected bone so brittle that it could break under slight stress (like a stumble or even going downstairs). As Aird wrote, he got the idea when reading the remark from *Leicester's Commonwealth* where it says that Amy fell without "hurting of her hood that stood upon her head." It was exactly to address this particular point that Aird made his suggestion.[2]

In recent years the breast cancer theory has come under attack in books and popular media which championed the newly-discovered head injuries as proofs for murder. On one TV show the forensic expert flatly dismissed Aird's cancer theory as speculative,[3] while in another TV programme an anthropologist made an experiment with lamb bones which did lend support to Aird's claims: The animal neck bone, although more robust than that of humans but hollowed out as if affected by cancer cells, did crumble under the amount of stress caused by even a short fall.[4]

---

1 Skidmore 2010 p. 222
2 Aird 1956 pp. 69–79
3 Allan Anscombe in *Elizabeth I: Killer Queen?*
4 Rose Drew, University of York, in *Mystery Files: The Virgin Queen*

Amy need not have suffered from breast cancer, however, her bones may have been weak for other reasons than cancer. Contrary to what is widely believed, osteoporosis occurs not just in postmenopausal women and elderly people. It can occur in otherwise healthy young women, often of slender built; the cause may vary from genetic to nutritional to idiopathic (of unknown cause).[1] A 27-year-old waitress slipped at work falling on her tailbone, thereby breaking her "spine bone in her upper back". Her spine bone density was low, while it was normal at the hip. The young woman suffered no lasting damage; she had never been pregnant or taken the Pill, but it was found that she had had no periods between 16 and 19 years of age, after splitting up with her boy friend. It was suggested that amenorrhea and anorexia in her teens were at the root of her problems.[2]

*

So, was Amy Dudley ill? The earliest known mention of her health is the one from 18 April 1559 in a dispatch of the Count de Feria to his master the King of Spain, that "she is very ill in one breast" ("está muy mala de un pecho"[3]). Shortly after, a Venetian diplomat in Brussels likewise wrote that Amy had "been ailing for some time", however as we have seen it is possible that he had his information from de Feria. De Feria, though, was related to the Sidneys and may have had first hand information.[4] De Feria's successor, de Quadra, also referred to Amy's health, observing that it had improved when she came to London in May 1559; apparently the Spanish court had few doubts that her health was precarious.

---

1 Ferrari et al. 2012
2 "Young Women and Osteoporosis"
3 Adams 1995 p. 63
4 See above p. 31.

At some point in 1559 Amy Dudley moved out from William Hyde's in Hertfordshire, where she had lived for at least two years. It was said that Hyde wanted her to leave because she "said she was poisoned, and for that cause he desired she might no longer tarry in his house."[1] What if she really believed she was poisoned, a very common phenomenon in the 16th century with people feeling unwell. (Jane Grey also believed her mother-in-law was poisoning her when she had caught a summer flu). Clearly, William Hyde wanted Amy to leave his house because he feared for his good name, but he may also have been tired of her hysterics.

Did Amy suffer from some illness of the mind? When interviewed by Thomas Blount, her maid, Mrs. Picto, said that her mistress had been "a good virtuous gentlewoman, and daily would pray upon her knees; and divers times she saith that she hath heard her pray to God to deliver her from desperation." – Asked if perhaps Amy had killed herself, Mrs. Picto's answer was: "No, good Mr. Blount ... do not judge so of my words; if you should so gather, I am sorry I said so much." Thomas Blount had known Amy, having accompanied her on some of her journeys,[2] but he was not a little puzzled:

> Certainly, my Lord, as little while as I have been here, I have heard divers tales of her that maketh me to judge her to be a strange woman of mind. ... It passeth the judgement of any man to say how it is, but truly the tales I do hear of her maketh me to think she had a strange mind in her: as I will tell you at my coming.

The people who wrote *Leicester's Commonwealth* in 1584

---
1   Adams, Archer, Bernard 2003b p. 66
2   Skidmore 2010 pp. 83, 145; Adams 1995 p. 102

claimed that Amy Dudley had been "sad and heavy", rejecting treatment for her "melancholy", while her husband's henchmen tried to poison her seeking the co-operation of Dr. Bayley of Oxford University, who however refused to mix her medicine with poison out of fear to be used as a scapegoat.[1] Now, a Dr. Walter Bayley really existed. He was admitted to medical practice in February 1559, and in 1561, the year after Amy's death, became Regius Professor of medicine at Oxford. He also happened to be Robert Dudley's trusted doctor and good friend for many years. He accompanied him to the spa waters at Buxton during the 1570s, and in 1578 Robert recommended him to the queen when she was suffering from severe toothache; three years later Bayley became one of her personal physicians.[2]

The authors of *Leicester's Commonwealth* knew quite well how unlikely it was for the Earl of Leicester to pass his holidays with the man who had refused to help him kill his wife, and so they made the absurd claim that the honest Dr. Bayley of 1560 was another "manner of man than he who now liveth about my Lord of the same name".[3] Of course there is not the slightest hint that Dr. Bayley had a doppelgänger who not only bore the same name but was, like him, "Professor of the Physic Lecture" at Oxford University. The question remains, though, why the authors of *Leicester's Commonwealth*, almost certainly exiled courtiers, included him in their story. Was it known that Robert Dudley had asked Dr. Bayley to treat Amy before her death? Was Philip Sidney alluding to Dr. Bayley when he wrote that it was foolish of the authors of the libel to put false words into the mouth of "persons yet alive"?[4]

As we have seen, in the late autumn of 1559 the two

---

1 Peck 1985 p. 64
2 Bakewell 2004; Skidmore 2010 p. 340
3 Peck 1985 p. 63
4 Jenkins 1961 p. 295; Adlard 1870 p. 67

Habsburg ambassadors (von Breuner and de Quadra) reported "veracious news" that Lord Robert was sending his wife poison. A "secret understanding" between queen and favourite was to ensure that Amy Dudley would be removed, von Breuner was convinced. In parallel, the special envoy of Emperor Ferdinand I was frantic to have Robert Dudley removed as well, so that Elizabeth could marry the Archduke Charles of Austria. It almost looks like the mentions of poison (of which the envoys of other countries seem never to have heard) had one source: Caspar von Breuner.[1] In the event though that they had a factual basis, or were based on more widespread rumours, they may also have meant "poisons" used as drugs; Robert may simply have sent his wife medicine.

Quite a few people seem to have believed that Amy Dudley would not have very long to live, as opposed to expecting her to be murdered. Was her husband among them? Much of his correspondence seems to have been lost and we simply cannot know the answer to this. His immediate reaction when Amy died in September 1560 was shock and possibly a suspicion that she might have killed herself. – The gossip of the times may add some clues: In March 1560 de Quadra had picked up that Lord Robert had "told somebody, who has not kept silence, that if he live another year he will be in a very different position from now. ... They say that he thinks of divorcing his wife."[2] This is the only mention of divorce in connection with their marriage, so perhaps what de Quadra heard could also have referred to Robert's knowledge of some serious illness of Amy's. The hostile *Journal* written within two years of her death claimed that among "the L. Rob. his men" it was rumoured "many times before ... that

---

1 See above pp. 33–34, 37.
2 CSP Simancas I p. 141

she was dead."[3] – If true, this can only mean that they expected her to die anytime soon.

Thomas Parry, Treasurer of the Household and highly trusted by Elizabeth, seems also to have believed this. He was known to be sympathetic towards a marriage of the queen with her favourite – until the scandal surrounding his wife's death, which made him "half ashamed for Lord Robert".[1] If he originally was in favour of the match, however, he must have believed that Robert would soon become a (scandal-free) widower.

Henry Hastings, 3rd Earl of Huntingdon, was Robert Dudley's brother-in-law and a pious and upright man. He added his condolences to a letter from Leicestershire on receipt of the news of Amy's death:

> My very good Lord.
> After my most hearty commendations.
> Although I am sure you are not without plenty of red deer, yet I am bold to send you half a dozen pies of a stag which was bred in the little garden at Ashby. I would be glad to understand how the baking doth like you, for I am in some doubt my cook hath not done his part, but you must pardon this fault, and it shall be amended: for if you love to eat of a stag, I will have one ready for you any time (I trust) this winter. It shall be as fat as any forest doth yield, and within four days warning he shall be sent to you. Thus my good lord and brother I take my leave, wishing to you in all things as to myself.
>
> From Leicester the 17 of Sept.
> Your assured brother to the end

---

[3] Adams, Archer, Bernard 2003b p. 66
[1] Skidmore 2010 p. 260; Froude 1911 pp. 208–209

H. Huntingdon.

As I ended my letter, I understood by letters the death of my lady your wife, I doubt not but long before this time you have considered what a happy hour it is, which bringeth man from sorrow to joy, from mortality to immortality, from care and trouble to rest and quietness, and that the Lord above worketh all for the best to them that love him well. I will leave my babbling and bid the buzzard cease to teach the falcon to fly and so end my rude postscript.

To my very good lord and brother, the Lord Robert Dudley.[1]

Huntingdon may not have been Robert Dudley's closest friend but Robert had planned to visit his sister and brother-in-law in the summer. He was quite emotionally close to his sister Katherine and stayed with her whenever Elizabeth would allow (which was not often). Huntingdon's comforting postscript has been much analyzed, and it is almost impossible to decide whether he was referring to Amy's expected death or the alarming death toll in Robert Dudley's family generally. He, however, certainly did not believe that Amy had been murdered.

---

1 Jackson 1878 p. 76

FIVE

SUICIDE?

When Sir Nicholas Throckmorton, Elizabeth's ambassador at the French court, heard of Lady Dudley's death, he instantly believed she had "by mischance broken her neck herself". He immediately became aware of his odd wording and corrected his letter before dispatching it, but suicide had undoubtedly crossed his mind.[1] Nicholas Throckmorton and his brothers about a decade earlier had been in the service of the Duke of Northumberland, Robert Dudley's father, and he till had close connections with the Dudleys, so we can assume that he knew Amy Dudley as well. He would at least have known something *about* her. Some contemporaries clearly suspected that she might have killed herself.

As we have seen, Thomas Blount suspected something when he came to Cumnor:

> Certainly, my Lord, as little while as I have been here, I have heard divers tales of her that maketh me to judge her to be a strange woman of mind. In asking of Picto what she might think of this matter, either chance or villainy, she said by her faith she doth judge very chance, and neither done by man nor by herself: For herself, she said, she was a good virtuous gentlewoman, and daily

---

1 Skidmore 2010 pp. 223–224

would pray upon her knees, and divers times she saith that she hath heard her pray to God to deliver her from desperation. Then, said I, she might have an evil toy in her mind. No, good Mr. Blount, said Picto, do not judge so of my words; if you should so gather, I am sorry I said so much.

My Lord, it is most strange that this chance should fall upon you. It passeth the judgement of any man to say how it is; but truly the tales I do hear of her maketh me to think she had a strange mind in her; as I will tell you at my coming.

What did Robert Dudley think? It seems likely that suicide crossed his mind as he was writing to Blount, having just received the news of his wife's death: "[P]raying you, even as my trust is in you, and as I have ever loved you, do not dissemble with me, neither let anything be hid from me, but send me your true conceit and opinion of the matter".

The coroner's inquest took its course, Thomas Blount making inquiries of his own, and after a few days he apparently was satisfied "that only misfortune hath done it and nothing else." He assured Robert though that "[m]yself will wait upon your Lordship to-morrow, and say what I know". Unfortunately, we do not know what that was.

*

The question remains whether Cumnor Place had adequate stairs to commit suicide. We do not know anything definite about the stairs leading up to Amy's chamber. Only one source, the *Journal*, claims that it had eight steps. However, as we have already mentioned and will discuss further down, this source is entirely based on rumour, and hostile rumour at that. The author had no access to Cumnor Place and clearly did not belong to the Dudley circle. Another staircase in the house was described as a newel staircase, but also as a sort of winder staircase,[1] and it is conceivable that Amy's staircase was similar, at the opposite side of the house. Still, nothing can really be said about the staircase leading to her chamber, and it cannot even be ruled out that Amy would have been able to jump from on high to the ground.

A suicide scenario more in keeping with the findings of the coroner's jury would be throwing herself down the stairs. This might seem an odd method to kill oneself, but it had the advantage to avoid the direct impression of suicide. It has also been suggested that Amy's fall might have been more of a distress signal than anything else, or that her body might have been moved in order to mislead the jurors.[2] As early as 1870, Amy's case has been interpreted as a possible case of parasuicide, the unconscious wish to kill oneself, or "an involuntary act of self-destruction", as it was phrased.[3] A modern coroner opined that "the 'ideation' of Amy's death, right down to the reaction of friends and relatives, fits the pattern of suicide precisely."[4] To commit suicide, no external causes are necessary, depression being a frequent cause. In Amy's case the separation from her husband – whom she seems to have loved – combined with the rumours about his relationship with the queen might have supplied a motive for suicide. We have already seen that she was a victim of Elizabeth's jealousy, as well as court gossip.[5] The *Journal* reports that "the people say she was killed by reason he forsook her company without cause and left her first at Hyde's house where she said she was poisoned, and for that cause he desired she might no longer tarry in his house."[6]

---

1 See above pp. 62–63.
2 Doran 1996 p. 44; Doran 2015 p. 124
3 Adlard 1870 p. 63
4 Gristwood 2007 p. 122
5 Adams, Archer, Bernard 2003b p. 66; Adams 2011
6 Adams, Archer, Bernard 2003b p. 66

These observations, if freed from the prejudiced perspective from which they were written,[1] may point to hysterical behaviour on Amy's part, to the "strangeness of mind" observed by Blount.

Suicide would also explain why Amy decided to send away all her servants to the fair at Abingdon and was "very angry" when Mrs. Odingsells insisted on staying. It is important to note that the coroner's report only says that she was alone in a chamber (almost certainly *her* chamber), not alone in the entire house, as is often said. That would be anyway unlikely, since Mrs. Odingsells was still there and the complex also housed Anthony Forster with his family and their servants, as well as the old Mrs. Owen. Furthermore, Amy had no problem with Mrs. Owen staying in the house and having dinner with her, which also speaks against the idea that she wanted to have the entire house empty.

*

How likely was it for a woman of Amy's class and age to commit suicide? Suicide was a serious crime in 16th century England and victims would be denied a Christian funeral; according to the law they were to be buried anonymously beside the road. The victim's heirs would be denied their inheritance, which would go to the crown. There was also the prospect to burn in hell, for to kill oneself was unforgivable according to church doctrine.

It is therefore regularly argued – not least in the case of Amy Dudley – that a young wealthy woman of that era would never commit suicide. So far the theory. What was 16th century reality like? The problem of public shame and anonymous burial could often be worked around by hushing up or ignoring the facts. Ophelia comes to mind. The

---

[1] Adams, Archer, Bernard 2003b p. 41

psychological mechanisms of religion are hard to fathom in any age. We simply do not know to what degree people were influenced by church teachings, how seriously they were taken by each individual. What we do know is that suicides were not a rare occurrence. There was a dramatic increase in suicides in England throughout the 16th century, setting in in the 1530s.[1]

---

[1] Murphy 1986 p. 259; MacDonald and Murphy 1993 p. 28

SIX

DISHONOURABLE REPORTS

On hearing the news of his wife's death, Robert Dudley retired to his house at Kew, "whither the lordes resorted to him to comfort him." His brother Ambrose and sister Mary also attended. This was noted by the author of the *Journal*, who however was not an eyewitness: "Himself, all his friends, many of the Lords and gentlemen, and his family be all in black, and weep dolorously, great hypocrisy used."[1]

His tailor's man, Jennings, came "to take measure of your lordship".[2] Lord Robert the mourning widower would wear "his blackes till Easter following", that is about six months.[3]

One of the first visitors at Kew after 10 September 1560, the day Robert probably arrived there, must have been William Cecil. Robert was exceedingly grateful and hoped that Cecil, as promised, would plead with Elizabeth for his return to court:

> Sir, I thank you much for your being hear, and the great frendshipp you have shewyd towardes me I shall not forgett. I am veary loath to wysh you hear againe, but I wold be very gladd to be with you thear. I pray you let me hear from you, what you think best for me to doe. If you dowbt, I pray you ask the questyon, for the soner you can

---

1   Adams; Archer; Bernard 2003b pp. 66–67
2   Adams 1995 p. 159
3   Adams; Archer; Bernard 2003b p. 67

80

advyse me thether, the more I shall thank you. I am sorry so sodden a chaunce shald breede me so great a chandge, for methinks I am hear all this while as it wear in a dreame, and to farr, to farre from the place I am bound to be, where, mythinkes also, this long, idle tyme can not excuse me for the dewty I have to discharge ells whear. I pray you help him that seues to be at liberty owt of so great bondage. Forgett me not, though you se me not, and I will remember you and fayll ye not, and so wysh you well to doe. In hast this morning.

I besech your Sir, forgett not to offer up the humble sacrafyce you promysed me.

Your veary assured,

R. Dudley[1]

As his manuscript shows, Robert was agitated when he penned this message: Instead of preparing a draft and writing out a "fair copy" afterwards he sent his letter with all his corrections, the writing looking rushed.[2] His state of shock is apparent: "for methinks I am here all the while as it were in a dream". This psychological fact cannot be faked; this is not the state of mind of a cold-blooded wife murderer. His single-minded preoccupation with getting back to court – his natural habitat – has been criticized ever since, but again it shows his genuine reaction. It did not occur to Robert to dissemble feelings which might have appeared more appropriate.

Was he visited by a dissembler? William Cecil certainly

---
1 Haynes pp. 361–362
2 Skidmore 2010 pp. 236, 238

had quickly capitalized on the tragedy which affected the man he may have seen as a rival for power. He had thrown oil into the flames of scandal by talking to the Spanish ambassador, the gossipy de Quadra, a few hours after the news of Amy Dudley's death had signalled to him that the queen might indeed marry her favourite and that his career might come to an end, or so he feared.

*

So, on a day in September 1560 William Cecil had a talk with Bishop de Quadra, the Spanish ambassador. On 28 July he had returned from Scotland,[1] where he had concluded the Treaty of Edinburgh, a triumph of diplomacy which guaranteed not only continued English influence on Scottish affairs, but also Elizabeth's right to her own throne. Still, Cecil was frustrated. He felt that his achievement went underappreciated while the queen was preoccupied with Lord Robert. In Scotland, rumours had come to his ears detailing how Elizabeth spent whole days with her favourite, "without coming abroad".[2] Now, some six months later, de Quadra reported once again the same thing:

> I met the Secretary Cecil, whom I know to be in disgrace. Lord Robert, I was aware, was endeavouring to deprive him of his place. With little difficulty I led him to the subject, and after my many protestations and entreaties that I would keep secret what he was about to tell me, he said that the Queen was going on so strangely that he was about to withdraw from her service. It was a bad sailor, he said, who did not make for port when he saw a storm coming, and for himself he

---
1 Read 1962 p. 192
2 Williams 1964 p. 60

perceived the most manifest ruin impending over the Queen through her intimacy with Lord Robert. The Lord Robert had made himself master of the business of the state and of the person of the Queen, to the extreme injury of the realm, with the intention of marrying her, and she herself was shutting herself up in the palace to the peril of her health and life. That the realm would tolerate the marriage, he said he did not believe. He was, therefore, determined to retire into the country although he supposed they would send him to the Tower before they would let him go. He implored me for the love of God to remonstrate with the Queen, to persuade her not utterly to throw herself away as she was doing, and to remember what she owed to herself and her subjects. Of Lord Robert he said twice that he would be better in paradise than here. ...

Last of all, he said that they were thinking of destroying Lord Robert's wife. They had given out that she was ill, but she was not ill at all; she was very well and taking care not to be poisoned. God, he trusted, would never permit such a crime to be accomplished or so wretched a conspiracy to prosper.[1]

If Cecil wanted to baffle de Quadra, he has certainly startled a number of historians. The Victorians were especially shocked, not so much because of Cecil's clairvoyance

---

1 Wilson 1981 pp. 115–116; Froude 1911 pp. 194–195. The Spanish original of the last paragraph reads: "y por oltimo me dixo que pensavan hazer morir a su muger de Roberto y que agora publicamente estava mala, pero que no estava sino muy buena y se guardava muy bien de ser envenenada y que nunca Dios permitira tan gran maldad, ni podria tener buen suceso tan mal negocio." (Lettenhove II p. 531).

regarding Amy's imminent murder, but because of the perceived involvement of Elizabeth. Martin Hume, who translated the materials in the *Spanish Calendar*, resorted to falsification: Instead of the original grammatical construction, *"pensavan hazer morir a su muger"*,[1] which can only be translated as "*they* were thinking of killing his wife", Hume wrote "*Robert* was thinking of killing his wife".[2] James Anthony Froude had also made transcriptions at the Spanish archives and was less afraid of what he saw there: "Last of all, he said that they were thinking of destroying Lord Robert's wife".

The question, of course, is who were "they"? The traditional interpretation is *Robert and Elizabeth*,[3] but the Spanish original is so vague that it is impossible to be sure who exactly Cecil thought was planning Amy Dudley's death.

This may well have been intentional on Cecil's part, though it is as likely a result of de Quadra's somewhat confusing composition. Did William Cecil really believe what he was saying? And, crucially, when did he speak to Philip II's agent? Many books have claimed that he met de Quadra on 6, or on 8 September, or certainly before the news of Amy's death reached the court. This is not because de Quadra's report would reveal a precise date, but because most Victorian and 20th century scholars could not imagine that Cecil was speaking anything but the truth. Indeed, all that can be established from de Quadra's text is that it reports events occurring on the days before and on 11 September 1560.[4] Amy died on 8 September and the first news of her death reached her husband on 9 September.

---

1 Lettenhove II p. 531
2 CSP Simancas I p. 175
3 Skidmore 2010 pp. 357–358 argues that "they" stands for Robert Dudley's henchmen.
4 For the complete letter in the original Spanish see Lettenhove II pp. 529–533.

After writing about his meeting with Cecil, de Quadra described how

> [t]he next day the Queen told me as she returned from hunting that Robert's wife was dead or nearly so, and asked me not to say anything about it.

And he finally added:

> Since writing the above I hear the Queen has published the death of Robert's wife, and said in Italian, "She broke her neck." She must have fallen down a staircase.[1]

From de Quadra's own words it is clear that Elizabeth spoke to him the day after his conversation with Cecil. He finished his letter on 11 September and later added a postscript, it is believed on the same day, after having heard the official news of Amy's death as given out by Elizabeth. It seems reasonable to assume that the official pronouncement would have followed hard on the queen's casual announcement to the ambassador that Amy "was dead or nearly so", perhaps on the next day. Thus, a very plausible date for Cecil's talk would be 9 September, the day the news reached the court's inner circle.

It is not likely that Cecil had prophetic gifts; it is much more plausible that he spoke to the ambassador after having gained knowledge of Amy's death before it was made public. Cecil did not want Robert Dudley as consort, not in 1560 and not later. Amy Dudley alive and well suited him best. Her death, on the other hand, would make her widower free to

---

1 CSP Simancas I pp. 175–176. "Despues de escrito esto ha publicado la Reina la muerte de Miladi Roberto, y ha dicho en italiano que *si ha rotto il collo*; deve de haver caydo de alguna escalera." (Lettenhove II p. 533).

marry the queen, at least in theory. Once Amy was no more, Cecil's best option was to add fuel to the fire of the incipient scandal.[1] In his view, and he was probably right, only a huge scandal could deter the queen from marrying the man she loved. Choosing de Quadra was the obvious thing to do – the Habsburg ambassadors had been the only ones who all along had suspected Robert and Elizabeth of foul play.

It could be argued, of course, that William Cecil really had knowledge in advance of a crime in the making and that, via de Quadra, he honestly wished to warn Elizabeth of her impending ruin. This was the view taken by de Quadra himself, who in the same letter prides himself on how the political players in England "would all confide in me if I mixed myself up in their affairs". Most probably Cecil exploited the ambassador's vanity here, however. If he would have had sensitive information touching Elizabeth he would surely have remembered her words to him at his appointment as Principal Secretary: "if yow shall knowe any thinge necessarye to bee declared to me of secresye yow shall show it to my self only".[2]

*

But Cecil had not just told de Quadra that Lady Dudley was about to be murdered, and taking great care not to be poisoned; significantly, he had added that "Lord Robert would be better in paradise than here." Cecil reckoned he could afford some sympathy, and correctly; the events brought his return to unquestionable favour and within weeks he had secured the position of Master of the Queen's Wards, a post that dealt with huge sums of money and must have been very welcome to such an ambitious builder of great ancestral homes as William Cecil.

---

1 Gristwood 2007 pp. 108–109; Skidmore 2010 p. 239
2 Doran 2013 p. 5

But it was not Cecil's intention to destroy Lord Robert completely. As we shall see, he and his colleague, Nicholas Throckmorton, worked hard to intrigue against another royal Dudley marriage, both men having been heavily implicated in a previous one. They had escaped unscathed, while Robert and his family had not, which was the principal reason they did not want him as consort. But both had known Robert for many years and had a good opinion of his person. Throckmorton explained to Cecil: "I do like him for some respects well, and esteem him for many good parts and gifts of nature that be in him."[1] – And Cecil wrote to Throckmorton: "I will never desire towards him but well."[2]

*

Nicholas Throckmorton was Elizabeth's ambassador in Paris and duly sent condolences to Robert Dudley on hearing of Amy's death: "My very good Lord, I understand of the cruel mischance late happened to my lady your late bedfellow, to your discomfort."[3]

Alas, what he heard at Paris in the following weeks made his "ears glow" and his hair stand on end. "My Lord," he informed the Marquess of Northampton, "I wish I were either dead, or that I were hence, that I might not hear the dishonourable and naughty reports that are here made of ye Queen's Majesty my gracious sovereign lady". Throckmorton was at his "wits end" what to answer those Frenchmen who "laugheth at us" saying "what religion is this that a subject shall kill his wife, and ye Prince not only bear withal but marry with him".[4]

A committed Protestant, Throckmorton feared for

---

1 Gristwood 2007 p. 112. Letter dated 28 September 1560.
2 Skidmore 2010 pp. 357–358; CSP Foreign 15 July 1561
3 Skidmore 2010 p. 243
4 Skidmore 2010 p. 243

England's prestige and security. He wrote frantic letters to Cecil, to Northampton, to Lord Admiral Clinton, to the Earl of Bedford, and the Earl of Pembroke. Like Cecil (and Lord Clinton), William Parr, Marquess of Northampton, was another member of the circle in power under Edward VI. A principal crony of Robert's father, the Duke of Northumberland, William Parr had narrowly escaped retribution at Queen Mary's hands and was still friends with Robert Dudley, or so it seemed. Among the presents exchanged between them were a nightingale and a crossbow for Lord Robert and a ring and money for the marquess.[1]

Alarmed, Throckmorton, again and again warned Northampton of the dire consequences for the commonwealth if Robert should marry the queen; and he thought it necessary to remind the marquess not to engage in the matter, to "be only a looker on", while yet his lordship would be wise if he could bring himself "to hinder it".[2]

*

Rumours were also circulating in England. Nine days after Amy's death, a Protestant preacher from Coventry decided he should demonstrate his loyalty by writing to Francis Knollys and William Cecil (his fellow Protestants) and inform them that "here in these Partes, seemeth unto me, to be a grevous, and dangerous suspicion, and muttering of the Death of her, which was the wife of my Lord Robert Dudlei." He announced the "displeasure of God" if there was no inquiry (he apparently was not aware of the coroner's inquest) and demanded "dew Ponishment, if any be founde guilte in this Mater", and that it "mai be openli known".[3]

When Throckmorton's first hysterical reports had arrived

---

1 Adams 1995 pp. 59, 158, 91, 169
2 Skidmore 2010 p. 249
3 Haynes p. 362

in England, his friend Henry Killigrew replied: "I cannot imagine what rumours they be you hear there, as you write so strange. Unless such were here of the death of my Lady Dudley; for that she brake her neck down a pair of stairs, which I protest unto you was only done by the hand of god, to my knowledge." After a few weeks he could imagine the rumours and added that "the Queen says she will make them false."[1]

Elizabeth indeed made clear that she had no doubts as to Amy's cause of death. On 27 November 1560, at Greenwich, she granted a private audience to Robert Jones, a special emissary sent by Nicholas Throckmorton. Jones' task was to convince Her Majesty that any thoughts of a wedding with Lord Robert were extremely dangerous. "When I came to touch nearer the quick," Jones informed Throckmorton, Elizabeth said "I have heard of this before," and that "he need not to have sent you withal". Jones then talked about Robert Dudley's "race", i.e. his unsuitable family background, "which I set forth in as vehement terms as the case required". When he pointed out that the Duke of Northumberland's "hatred" had been directed rather

> to her than to the Queen her sister, she laughed, and forthwith turned herself to the one side and to the other, and set her hand upon her face. She thereupon told me, that the matter had been tried in the country, and found to be contrary to that which was reported, saying that he was then in the Court, and none of his at the attempt at his wife's house; and that it fell out as should neither touch his honesty nor her honour.[2]

Elizabeth ended by saying that "my Ambassador knoweth

---
1   Skidmore 2010 p. 244
2   Hardwicke SP p. 165

somewhat of my mind in these matters." Obviously, she had informed Throckmorton of her thoughts about Amy's case in a letter which has not survived.

The word *attempt*, as Jones reported it, has caused raised eyebrows, while the preceding words have been overlooked: *none of his*, that is Robert's men, were "at the attempt at his wife's house". If taken literally, the queen would have been referring to an assault by a third party; it is also possible that it was a slip of the tongue, or that the over-assiduous Jones misremembered Elizabeth's words, as does happen all the time when one reports speech by memory.

As Jones reported to Throckmorton, he had also a talk with Cecil about the rumours concerning Amy, and especially about some remarks made by the Queen of France, Mary Stuart. The content of these alleged remarks found their way to Robert, who was not at all pleased and also had a talk with Jones:

> The 26th of November all my Lords of the Council dined at the Scotch Ambassador's lodging, where they were very highly feasted. I repaired thither to shew myself to my Lords, where, after I had attended half dinner time, my Lord Robert rose up, and went to the Court, and in the way sent a gentleman back to will me to repair thither after him, as I did ... Being come unto him, he asked me, whether the French Queen had said that the Queen's Majesty would marry her horse-keeper, and told me ... that Mr. Secretary told him that the French Queen had said so. I answered, that I said no such matter. He laid the matter upon me so strong ... I would not deny, that the French Queen had said that the Queen would marry the Master of her horses. This was all he said to me, and he willed me that I should

in no case let it be known to Mr. Secretary that he had told me thus much, as I have not indeed, nor mean not to do; whereby I judge that Mr. Secretary did declare it only to the Queen, at whose hands my Lord Robert had it.[1]

When he had returned to court in October, the *Journal* reported, Lord Robert was "in great hope to marry the queen, for she maketh such appearance of good will to him." The writer observed that "[h]e giveth her many presents" and that his men talked about the marriage as if it were already concluded. Many lords were always at Lord Robert's heels.[2]

Throckmorton's man, Robert Jones, had one further talk on the evening of the day he spoke to Elizabeth, to Henry Killigrew, who "said in the end unto me with, as it were, a sad look, I think verily, that my Lord Robert shall run away with the hare, and have the Queen; to whom I answered nothing."[3]

*

Indeed, at London "the Reporte whas that hyr Hygness shoolde marry him".[4] Elizabeth, for her part, began to realize that this was what she could not risk to do. According to what Cecil told de Quadra in October, she had decided not to marry Lord Robert.[5] As usual, though, she could not quite make up her mind. At the end of November she was about to ennoble Robert by making him a duke, an essential part of his becoming royal consort. However:

---

1 Hardwicke SP p. 164
2 Adams, Archer, Bernard 2003b p. 67
3 Hardwicke SP p. 164
4 Doran 1996 p. 45
5 CSP Simancas I p. 177

The Queen's Majesty stayeth the creation. The bills were made for the purpose, at the day appointed. When they were presented, she with a knife cut them asunder. I can by no means learn, and yet I have talked with such as know much, that my Lord Robert's matters will not go, as was looked for; and yet the favours be great which are shewed him at the Queen's Majesty's hands.[1]

Another Englishman who hoped to marry the queen was Henry Fitzalan, 19th Earl of Arundel. Arundel had been a principal enemy of the Duke of Northumberland, but before Amy's death his relations with Robert Dudley had been well enough, Robert's account books showing visits and the exchange of presents.[2] In September 1561, though, a month after the coroner's verdict of Amy Dudley's case was officially passed, de Quadra heard that Arundel had "had such words" with Lord Robert "that the Earl went home". Hoping to find incriminating evidence against his rival, Arundel started "drawing up copies of the testimony given in the inquiry respecting the death of Lord Robert's wife." The Spanish ambassador gleefully reported how "Robert is now doing his best to repair matters as it appears that more is being discovered in that affair than he wished."[3]

It is important to note, though, that apparently nothing was discovered. Arundel ("and others", according to de Quadra) did simply not find anything suspicious in the documents. The true reason why the earl and his aristocratic friends were so keen on destroying Lord Robert's marriage prospects had little to do with Robert's deceased wife. They were alarmed that if Elizabeth indeed married her favourite, "there will

---

1   Harwicke SP p. 168
2   Adams 1995 pp. 84, 154
3   CSP Simancas I p. 213

rysse troble amonge the noblemen," as one of Arundel's men, Arthur Guntor, put it. Regarding Lord Robert, he said:

> I thowght hym to be the causse that my lorde my master myght not marry the Quene's Hyghnes; wherfor I woolde that he had bene put to dethe with his father, or that some roffen [ruffian] woolde have dyspached hym by the way as he hath gone, with some dagge[r] or gonne.[1]

Guntor also warned that in case of Robert's marriage with the queen, the former would no doubt "remember eny owlde matter passed heartoforre", which of course would be "to my lord my master's dyspleasurre and hynderance".

That men like Arundel feared Robert Dudley's revenge was also hinted at by Pope Pius IV (who had also heard the news from England): "The greater part of the nobility of that island take ill the marriage which the said queen designs to enter with the Lord Robert Dudley ... they fear that if he becomes king, he will want to avenge the death of his father, and extirpate the nobility of that kingdom." The pope explained to his listeners that Elizabeth countered such notions saying that Lord Robert "was of a very good disposition and nature, not given by any means to seek revenge of former matters past".[2]

---

1 Haynes p. 365
2 Adams 2002 p. 165

SEVEN

MURDER?

The first reports about Amy Dudley's murder were written ten months before her death. We have seen how the Habsburg ambassadors, de Quadra and von Breuner, wrote home about a supposed agreement between the queen and Lord Robert to poison his wife and then get married. There were also stories that Elizabeth was pregnant by Robert Dudley, and many people were certainly inclined to believe all sorts of gossip. The host of the inn Thomas Blount stayed at said, regarding Amy's death, that "some were disposed to say well and some evil". He was probably right.

The author of the *Journal* that we have already quoted may have been the MP John Hales.[1] Hales was a fierce Protestant and in the reign of Edward VI had been an advisor to the Duke of Somerset. He had been behind Somerset's so-called social policy and significantly he had also clashed with John Dudley, Robert's father, over (unrealistic) reform plans. The *Journal*'s author did not know Robert Dudley personally, as he writes, but he is strikingly hostile towards all of the Dudley family.[2] It is no wonder he was among those who believed that Robert Dudley had killed his wife.

The *Journal of Matters of State* or *BL Additional MS 48023* is a draft collection of material for a history that was never completed. The manuscript was found in an English archive in about 1978 and it contains a few passages that

---

1 Admas, Archer, Bernard 2003b pp. 45–51
2 Admas, Archer, Bernard 2003b p. 41

have become the principal source in support of the murder theory:

> Howe the Lorde Roberte's wief brake her necke at Foster's howse in Oxfordshire in the natiuitatis Marie A 1560, her gentellwomen being gon forth to a fier. Howebeyt yt was thought she was slayne, for Sir —— Varnye was there that daie and whyleste the deade was doing was goinge over the fier and tarried there for his man, who at leingthe cam, and he saied, thowe knave, whye tarieste thowe? He answered, shoulde I com before I had don? Haste thowe don? Quoth Verney. Yea, quoth the man, I have made hytt sure. So Verney cam to the courte.[1]

So, here we have a report of how Amy's putative killers proceeded and what they talked. There have been differing interpretations, however, of where exactly Sir —— Varnye (without doubt Sir Richard Verney) was on 8 September 1560. From reading the text it might appear that Verney himself was at Cumnor and impatiently stayed there until his man met up with him after doing the deed. It depends on how to interpret the word "fier". Norman Jones believed it meant a "fire" (at Cumnor),[2] while most other historians seem to read it as a "fair" – a reference to the fair at Abingdon. In this reading of the text Verney would apparently have come first to Cumnor, but would then have gone to the fair at Abingdon to wait for his servant.

Of course, the latter interpretation is better in accord with the known facts of Amy's last day, namely that she sent her

---

1 Adams, Archer, Bernard 2003b p. 66. *Natiuitate Marie* is Latin for the Narivity of Mary, a religious feast celebrated on 8 September, the day Amy died.
2 Jones 1993 p. 127

"people" to pass the day at the fair at Abingdon. On the other hand, if the author of the *Journal* meant an actual fire to which Amy's "gentlewomen" had gone to watch it, this would be at odds with the facts as we know them from the letters of Thomas Blount to Robert Dudley.

From the *Journal* it is clear that its author was based in London, although he cannot have been very much at court in the first two years of Elizabeth's reign. He did not recognize Robert Dudley, a very prominent court figure, when the latter passed by him in October 1560, a month or so after Amy's death.[1]

Whatever the author meant concerning Verney's whereabouts, he was reporting hearsay. It would be typical for information spread by word of mouth that basic facts like the absence of Amy's servants were reported in variations. The author, clearly, was not at either Cumnor or Abingdon, neither on 8 September nor later, and so he could not have heard what Verney and his man were speaking, and anyway it is extremely unlikely that the two would have had witnesses who overheard what they said.

Clearly, stories about Sir Richard Verney going to Cumnor on 8 September 1560 circulated in court circles, for the authors of *Leicester's Commonwealth*, written in 1584 some 20 years after the *Journal* was written, elaborated on this story. Presumably the authors of this pamphlet did not draw on the *Journal*,[2] as it was apparently never completed, nor widely circulated.

In the murder story as told by *Leicester's Commonwealth* Sir Richard Verney "by commandment remained with her that day alone, with one man only," and forcibly sends her servants away, "to a market two miles off". Amy is buried twice over, first secretly at Cumnor parish church, then at Oxford, so that her husband may play the grieving widower.

---

1   Adams, Archer, Bernard 2003 p. 67. See above p. 64.
2   Adams, Archer, Bernard 2003 p. 66

Meanwhile, the inquest's verdict is murder, not misfortune or accidental death. Richard Verney's servant, who had witnessed Amy's murder, ends up in prison "for a felony in the marches of Wales". "[O]ffering to publish the manner of the said murder," he is killed before he can tell the story:

> And Sir Richard himself, dying about the same time in London, cried piteously and blasphemed God, and said to a gentleman of worship of mine acquaintance not long before his death that all the devils in hell did tear him in pieces. The wife also of Bald Buttler, kinsman to my Lord, gave out the whole fact a little before her death.[1]

The identity of this "gentleman of mine acquaintance" is not revealed, although it has been suggested that "Bald Butler" and his wife pop up in Robert Dudley's papers and in Amy's funeral procession.[2] The question remains, of course, how Mrs. Butler had acquired her first hand knowledge of what went on at Cumnor on that Sunday. It is unlikely that Verney would have told her.

Robert Dudley had distant relatives called Butler.[3] There was also Anthony Butler, MP, of Coates, Lincolnshire (1522–1570). Anthony became a very wealthy man due to transactions with the Court of Augmentations in the 1540s and 1550s, and he was also active in short term speculations with rents, as well as other money matters. At this time he served another MP, Sir John Williams, but in his will of 1570 he wrote of "my very good lord and master my lord the Earl of Leicester".[4] Robert Dudley, in his turn, applied for the

---

1 Peck 1985 p. 58
2 Skidmore 2010 pp. 370–371. See above p. 60.
3 Peck 1985 p. 131
4 Baker 1982

wardship of Charles Butler, Anthony's son, as a favour to "my old servant".[1]

Anthony Butler first appears in Robert Dudley's household accounts in 1559, when he received 40s "at his departing into the country after the coronation".[2] Two months after Amy's demise he appears again:

> Paid unto Anthonny Butteler the xvj daye of November for the discharge of a bounde in the which Thomas Blunt esquier stoode bounde unto the said Anthonny Butteler Cli.[3]

It has, of course, been suggested that Anthony Butler may have been "Bald Butler" and that those £100 constituted hush money from Robert Dudley.[4] In view of the fact that this sum was repayment for a bond "in the which Thomas Blount ... stood bound unto", this transaction seems not particularly ominous. We have already seen that Anthony Butler was a man who heavily dealt in money matters, apparently as a business model.

A similar case is Robert Dudley's payment of £719 about the same time to "Francis Barthewe stranger for monney due unto him by your lordship for the which Anthonny Forster stood bound".[5] Another suspicious transaction related to Amy's death has been detected here; however, Francis Barthewe (or Bartie) was a Flemish merchant to whom Robert had been owing money for some five years, including debts heaped up by his mother, the Duchess of Northumberland. According to a surviving bill, Barthewe

---

1 Adams 1995 p. 465
2 Adams 1995 p. 47
3 Adams 1995 p. 125
4 Skidmore 2010 p. 371
5 Adams 1995 p. 125

also supplied Robert with all sorts of commodities between 1559 and 1566.[1]

As for the wife of Bald Butler, it has been suggested that she may have been Anthony Butler's wife, but again, this is mere speculation, and Amy's funeral was attended by two Mrs. Butlers, the elder and the younger.[2] Finally, Robert Dudley mentioned two Butlers in his will.[3]

It may be added that according to *Leicester's Commonwealth* Bald Butler was Robert Dudley's kinsman, however Anthony Butler seems not to have been one of those. *Leicester's Commonwealth* is a work of satire and, as we have seen, only loosely based on fact. It is also fictional, taking the form of a dialogue between a Cambridge scholar, a lawyer, and a gentleman. The political context of the work is to be seen in the events leading up to the final nemesis of Mary Queen of Scots. The work's underlying agenda is the succession of Mary to the English throne. She was at that time deeply embroiled in various plots against Elizabeth's life, and the English queen's councillors were keen to find a way to get rid of this threat once and for all. Robert Dudley, Earl of Leicester, one of those councillors, was indeed the most exalted patron of a militant Protestant foreign policy. It is not a surprise therefore that the outstanding feature of *Leicester's Commonwealth* is an all-round attack on him. Among other things, he is presented as an "atheist" and a "dictator" who terrorizes a helpless queen and is himself engaged in a long-term conspiracy to snatch the crown from Elizabeth.

After his first exercise in murder – that of his wife with the assistance of Sir Richard Verney – Leicester continues his murderous work with the expert help of his Italian physician, Dr. Giulio. The husbands of his lovers Lady Douglas

---

1 Adams 1995 p. 40
2 Adlard 1870 p. 54
3 Peck 1985 p. 137

Sheffield and Lettice, Countess of Essex, are removed by poison, as are the Cardinal of Chatillon, Nicholas Throckmorton, and Lady Margaret Douglas. The Earl of Sussex is also dispatched, in the same manner, and Leicester even pays Francis Drake to kill Thomas Doughty during the circumnavigation of the world. (The real Thomas Doughty was executed by Drake for mutiny at sea).

The authorship of this monstrous pamphlet is much debated among scholars, but it is clear that it was written by disgruntled exiled English courtiers in France with strong sympathies for the Catholic cause; it was quite possibly a group effort. As we have seen, the book has been used as evidence that Amy was murdered, but the inconsistencies with the two principal sources of what happened to her – the coroner's report and the correspondence between Robert Dudley and Thomas Blount – are considerable.

Some of these have already been mentioned,[1] yet even the discrepancies between *Leicester's Commonwealth* and the *Journal* are significant. For example, the coroner's jury's verdict in the *Journal* is accident, while *Leicester's Commonwealth* claims it was murder.[2] Also, Verney in the *Journal* is at Cumnor only on the day of Amy's death, while in *Leicester's Commonwealth* he seems to be living there. A thing that both these principal sources for the murder theory have in common is Sir Richard Verney. Who was that man?

*

The year of birth of Sir Richard Verney, of Compton Verney in Warwickshire, is unknown, but documents show that he served in the household of Robert Dudley's father in the 1540s and 1550s. So may, indeed, have his wife, for in 1553 a "Mrs. Verney" was listed among six salaried gentlewomen

---
1   See above p. 96.
2   Peck 1985 p. 64

of the Duke of Northumberland.[1] In 1549 Verney received velvet shoes from John Dudley, Lord Lisle, Robert's elder brother, as well as "a Spanish jerkin guarded with velvet". The favour was reciprocated with "a dagger that Sir Richard Verney gave my lord"; however, "the same was stolen out of the chamber at Westminster."[2]

From about the late 1530s until his downfall in 1553, the Duke of Northumberland had been the leading landowner in the counties of the West Midlands. After Elizabeth's accession in 1558, Northumberland's former clientele began to regroup under the leadership of his surviving sons, Ambrose and Robert, but especially Robert. Sir Richard Verney was among the gentlemen who could hope for advancement.[3] In 1559–1560 Robert held the lord-lieutenantship of Warwickshire and Worcestershire jointly with Sir Ambrose Cave. Cave suggested Richard Verney to Lord Robert as deputy, as "a gentleman meet to serve in that behalf [who] would willingly endeavour himself for Warwickshire if it please you to appoint him or require him by your letters to take the charge upon him."[4]

As it turned out, Lord Robert decided that John Fisher, of Packington, was the right man for the deputy job, but he still thought Verney to be a good host for his wife, Amy. As we have seen, Amy moved to Compton Verney sometime in 1559, probably the summer. In September 1559 Robert Dudley's account book recorded "ij peir of hose sent to my ladye by Sir Richard Vernies servant."[5]

The *Journal* explained that she had complained about being poisoned at William Hyde's house, "and for that cause he desired, she might no longer tarry in his house. From

---

1   Loades 1996 p. 305
2   HMC Second Report pp. 102, 101
3   Adams 2002 pp. 163–164
4   HMC Bath V p. 142
5   Adams 1995 pp. 92, 381–383

thence she was removed to Verney's house in Warwickshire, and so at length to Forster's house."[1] Her arrival at Cumnor by December 1559 is suggested by "ij y.[ards] of blew sowing sylke sent to my ladie by Mr Forster".[2]

The author of the *Journal*, who may have been the MP John Hales, has nothing good to say about Verney. Hales had been very active in Warwickshire at the time of John Dudley's ascendancy in county affairs, and, as we have seen, in 1548 the two men had clashed over Hales' reform agenda. So it is quite possible that Hales knew Sir Richard Verney from his Warwickshire days, and it is equally possible that he harboured some grudge against him, for he certainly did not like the man. He writes that "many times" before Amy's death, "it was bruited by the L. Rob. his men that she was dead", and that "[t]his Verney and divers his servants used before her death, to wish her death, which made the people to suspect the worse."[3]

It is of course possible that Verney was impatiently counting the days until Amy's death by natural causes, however the writer seems to imply that Verney and other of Lord Robert's men were bragging about their planned misdeed. While the most likely explanation for the *Journal*'s statement is that Verney and others expected Amy to die sometime soon, the question also arises how Hales (or whoever the author may have been) knew Verney's thoughts and what he was talking. Judging from his one surviving letter, Verney seems not to have left Warwickshire in those months, and the *Journal*'s author was certainly London-based.

*

---

1 Adams, Archer, Bernard 2003b p. 66
2 Adams 1995 pp. 106, 382
3 Adams, Archer, Bernard 2003b p. 66

Did Verney – unsuccessful for the time being in his bid for a major office in county administration – try to advance himself by more sinister means? Did he really travel to Berkshire in order to ingratiate himself with his master by ridding him of a cumbersome wife? Would he not have seen the consequences, the ensuing scandal that ruined any chances of Lord Robert marrying the queen? Would he have risked to be seen entering and leaving Cumnor Place in broad daylight – the largest house on the spot, next the parish church? Or was he simply travelling through Abingdon on the day of Amy's death, the *Journal* saying that he came to London afterwards? Such a coincidence could well explain his subsequent association with the events at Cumnor, and his presence in London would likely have been noticed, for he was apparently not a frequent visitor of the court.

On 20 April 1560, about five months before the tragedy at Cumnor, Verney wrote a letter to Robert Dudley, from Warwick:

> I am very sorry that I cannot, according to your Lordship's expectation and my duty, make my repair presently towards you for two principal causes. The one health, which I possess not as I could wish. The other wealth, which doth not abound in me as perhaps is thought. But as it is both I and all things else mine are and always shall be to my best power advanced in any your affair or commandment when opportunity offereth. I am sorry also to write unto your Lordship the late mishap and loss by death of one cast of hawks which my cousin Davers whom I preferred to your Lordship's service had in keeping. But like as I know your Lordship can best consider that casual things have many times such casual end, so I have good hope you will

please to let them pass, and to think no wilful negligence in your man, who I assure you taketh the mischance marvellous grievously. Except your Lordship by your letters seem something to comfort him, I believe it will do him hurt. He grieveth a great deal the more that they should miscarry in his guiding considering that he hath had knowledge and long experience of the keeping of hawks.[1]

A man fussing over the embarrassing fact of a few deceased hawks: Is this the man who would risk to murder his patron's wife? In her own house, so that suspicion would immediately fall on Lord Robert and "his men", men like Verney? Sir Richard Verney was never arrested or otherwise molested by the authorities – which seems odd if his putative crime were much talked about. Nor was he ever mentioned by foreign ambassadors, all keenly interested in rumours relating to Lord Robert and his wife. Life went on as usual for Sir Richard Verney; and he was scandal-free enough to serve as Sheriff of Warwickshire in 1562.[2]

We have seen that, evidently, Robert Dudley was shocked by his wife's death when it came. Had he suspected Verney of killing her, he would doubtlessly have sought to prosecute him, not least to clear himself of any suspicion. Instead he seems to have remained on friendly terms with Verney until the latter's death in about 1568.[3] In the 1570s, Robert Dudley was even concerned about the well-being of Richard Verney's orphaned little grandson.

Verney's son George had been a spendthrift and when he died the Earl of Leicester applied for the wardship of his young son from the Master of the Court of Wards, William

---

1 HMC Bath V p. 156
2 Adlard 1870 p. 87
3 Skidmore 2010 p. 358

Cecil, Lord Burghley. Wardship, according to a Victorian authority, "would give him the profits of the lands till the heir should reach the age of twenty-one. It was an arrangement which, at the same time, would be accounted a favor shown to the heir, as taking him out of the hands of the officers of the Crown and leaving him in the care of a friend of his late father",[1] which, in this case, would probably mean grandfather.

Two letters from Leicester to Burghley survive about this case; William Cecil and Robert Dudley were by that time very regular correspondents:

> My very good Lord,
>
> I have thought good to let you understand, that where of late I sent unto your Lordship, my solicitor, Nutthall, touching the lands of young Varney, by reason there is hitherto no order taken, nor any man appointed for the looking thereunto, both the lands and the house go to much rack, and if speedy remedy be not provided, it cannot but greatly turn to the loss and harm of the child. The meadows stand yet undealt withal, whereby the hay of the ground is like to be utterly spoiled, for want of some that should look to the inning of it. And I, for my part, albeit divers have called upon me (for that your Lordship granted unto me the wardship of the child), to take some order in it, yet have forborne still to do anything, expecting some direction from your Lordship. And now very lately I understand by Sir Thomas Lucy, there be divers that offer to make entries upon the land by virtue of statutes and other foolish bonds

---

1 Adlard 1870 p. 93

made by his father in his lifetime; wherein your Lordship is to take some speedy order, otherwise it cannot but turn to the child's undoing, or extreme prejudice, at the least.

But not perceiving any man appointed, neither yet any of his friends very willing to meddle with the land, considering how foolishly the late father hath left the whole encumbered, I have thought good for the young child's sake to put your Lordship in remembrance, that the matter, in time for his more benefit hereafter, may be looked into presently, which if your Lordship cannot find any that will carefully deal for him, I will myself take what charge thereof you will require or appoint, upon the survey of such as your Lordship shall assign for it, which for the poor child's sake, I pray your Lordship may be in as convenient time as the cause requireth, for all goeth almost to spoil. And so I wish your Lordship right heartily to fare well.

From Woodstock this 30th of July, 1574.

Your Lordship's most assured,
R. Leicester[1]

Notwithstanding the efforts of Sir Thomas Lucy, young Richard Verney's uncle on his mother's side and a man knighted by Robert Dudley and chiefly known to us for allegedly imprisoning a youth named William Shakespeare for poaching, there was still no progress made about the Verney estate almost a year later. On 16 June 1575, Leicester

---

1   Adlard 1870 pp. 92–93

returned to the issue in another letter to Burghley in which he also explained why he had desired the Verney wardship "only for the good of that house, knowing that he was likely to receive else much harm". The duties of a legal guardian also included to find a marriage partner for the ward (and usually make some money out of that), so Leicester

> was desirous and willing to make offer of his marriage to your Lordship for one of Mr. Cave's daughters, your nieces, before any other, so am I still desirous that match should take place, as well for the good worship of the house as chiefly the alliance with your Lordship, by whose means he may receive his greatest benefit, and because your Lordship shall perceive my meaning was wholly for the young child's benefit ... even as I offered his match in marriage with your Lordship, ... so did I as freely offer all other things that were to be looked unto of his to Sir Thomas Lucy, his uncle, who I know hath loved the father and grandfather, and would willingly further this, yet upon perusing the state of things as they stand, would by no means deal with them, neither take the charge of them.
>
> I offered likewise to any other of his nearest kin the same with all commodities that they would make or that I could procure, at your Lordship's hands, for them, also that his house and other things might be well-governed and preserved for the young man. There was none would meddle with them ... and without your lordship sets your favourable help hereafter, as occasion shall serve justly, the boy shall scant, while he lives, be able to keep the countenance of a mere gentleman, and

yet is his living worth together well a thousand marks a year.

But his father, the unthrift, that your Lordship and I had so much to do withal, hath made such bargains and leases, and in debt £2000 when he died, whereby except the young boy find good friends, when he comes to man's estate, he shall have all his lands subject to bonds and forfeitures.

Leicester therefore had instructed Sir John Huband "to take it in hand", that some of the young Verney's debts "may in this time be paid, and so the child less burdened hereafter". In short, Robert Dudley was concerned about the child's education and future: "Sir John hath great care in bringing him up, and so have I chiefly, till he be a little bigger to go to some other place to get more knowledge; and as hitherto he hath had no allowance for him, so my request to your Lordship is that you will appoint him some reasonable portion, which I dare undertake at the least shall be employed toward him every way."[1]

So, uncharacteristically for the system, this wardship brought with it only costs for Robert Dudley.[2] The whole episode shows that the Earl of Leicester valued and remembered the deceased Richard Verney as a good man; it does not look like the reward for murder.

*

Murder, in Elizabethan England, was a rare occurrence. As opposed to manslaughter and the occasional "bloudie robberie", "wilful murther" with "malice aforethought" made up only about 5% of indicted felonies in the courts of assize,

---
1   Adlard 1870 pp. 93–95
2   Haynes 1987 p. 124

and, interestingly, "killing one's spouse was ... not a common type of murder" according to surviving statistics.[1]

The eminent legal commentator and civil servant, Sir Thomas Smith, believed murder by poison to be as good as non-existent in England. Indeed, in chronicles such as Holinshed's and in pamphlet literature, "a severe blow to the head followed by the cutting of the unconscious or semi-conscious victim's throat" was the classic murder method. The use of knives and daggers was somewhat less common, while poison (Sir Thomas Smith notwithstanding) was the preserve of the female perpetrator. Details thought to be suspicious were important clues – such as rushes of straw that had been suddenly exchanged or a body found without wounds but with a broken neck.[2]

Many coroner's juries in the 16th century were doubtlessly influenced, either by connections of perpetrators or relatives of victims, or both.[3] It should be noted that it was not just Robert Dudley's steward Thomas Blount who was around during the inquest into Amy's death, but also her two half-brothers and "other her friends". Importantly, though, none of these persons was in the vicinity of Cumnor, the place she died, when the jury assembled.

According to his own notes, William Cecil manipulated the case of a cook killed in his household by his son-in-law the 17th Earl of Oxford. On Cecil's pressure a London jury found that the cook had committed suicide, by the odd method of running into Oxford's rapier.[4] On the other hand, when the 4th Duke of Norfolk's pistol went off in a riding accident and killed one of his retainers the case was correctly judged as manslaughter (while the duke was pardoned).[5]

---

1 Bellamy 2005 pp. 1, 2
2 Bellamy 2005 pp. 1, 11, 13, 14
3 Bellamy 2005 p. 32
4 Nelson 2003 pp. 47, 152
5 Williams 1964 p. 33

There have also been differing interpretations of Christopher Marlowe's violent death in a tavern, and there is a real danger to suspect every inquest to have been manipulated as soon as interesting people are involved.[1]

It is sometimes implied that the death of Amy Dudley was not "fully investigated". However, Elizabethan coroner's juries were perfectly capable of basic detective work like surveying the crime scene and questioning neighbours and witnesses. Depositions would then be recorded and influence the juries' verdicts; unfortunately, few such documents seem to have survived.[2] Coroner's juries also regularly considered medical evidence before rendering verdicts, relying both on expert witnesses and "their own knowledge of medicine, which was often extensive and reliable". It is also believed that they were capable of investigating suicides and accidental deaths as thoroughly as homicides.[3]

Thomas Blount reported that the jury members were very diligent and, some being "very enemies" of Anthony Forster, were anything but slack:

> Whether equity of the cause or malice to Forster do forbid it, I know not, they take great pains to learn the truth. ... They be very secret; and yet do I hear a whispering that they can find no presumptions of evil. And if I may say to your Lordship my conscience, I think some of them may be sorry for it, God forgive me.

It has been pointed out that some of the jurors in Amy's case may have had doubts about the verdict of "misfortune". This has been inferred from the last words of the verdict: "[A]nd the jurors say on their oath that the aforesaid Lady Amy in

---

1 Bossy 2006
2 Bellamy 2005 pp. 16, 24
3 Loar 2010

the manner and form aforesaid by misfortune came to her death and not otherwise, *as they are able to agree at present*".[1] However, this very likely indicates a formulaic option to change their minds at a later date rather than a covert expression of dissent.

---

1 Skidmore 2010 p. 233; TNA KB 9/1073/f.80. The original Latin phrase reads *"prout eis ad presens constare potest"*.

Figure 2: Robert Dudley, Earl of Leicester, 1560s. (Courtesy Yale Center of British Art).

EIGHT

OLD BOYS

In May 1566 Robert Dudley, Earl of Leicester, gave "four ells of black taffeta for a short gown and three yards of black velvet to guard the same ... to Mr. Smith the Queen's man".[1] The *Journal* describes the coroner's jury's foreman as "one Smith ... who was the Queen's man being Lady Eliz." and who was sacked for his "lewd behaviour". This must have been Richard Smythe, a "burgess of Abingdon".[2] It has been claimed that the Smith of the black taffeta was the same Smith as Smith the foreman – and that this somehow proves that the jury six years earlier had been bribed.[3]

If one reads the order to present Smith with valuable stuffs in context, however, it is immediately clear that he was only one of the persons receiving them:

> Mr. Pecock I pray you delyver to thys berer foure elles of blak taffata for a shorte gowne and thre yards of blak vellet to gard the same whyche gowne my lord dothe gyve to Mr. Smythe the quenes man. and also iij yards quarter of crymsen satten for a dublet whyche my lord gyvythe to the Mayre of Abynglon and vij yards of blak satten for ij dubletts whyche my lord gyvythe to ij of the mayres brethern of the towne of Abyngton.

---
1 Skidmore 2010 p. 369
2 Skidmore 2010 p. 210
3 Skidmore 2010 pp. 369–370; Bernard 2000 pp. 170–171

thys hartely fare you well, thys xvi of May 1566.
yrs Antho: Forster.[1]

The background to this gift of robes was Robert Dudley's appointment as High Steward of Abingdon in the same year, 1566. Smith had served as Mayor of Abingdon the previous year, 1565, and was obviously still a member of the corporation. The stuffs were delivered under the supervision of Anthony Forster – like many other items to make clothes of, to a number of people, and it seems Robert Dudley gifted such stuffs on a fairly regular basis.[2]

There may even have been a connection to the queen's visit to Oxford University in the summer of 1566. The Earl of Leicester had become Chancellor of the university in 1564, and in 1566 he was Elizabeth's official host. It was a grand reception, one venue being St. Mary's Church,[3] Amy's resting place. Beforehand, Robert was naturally busy making sure the occasion would be a success by all standards. Richard Smythe, alongside his brethren of the town council of Abingdon, may have been the sort of people who might be expected to attend; they would have needed the right outfit (and of course Robert may have been grateful for a convenient outcome of the inquest).

The first time he had heard of Mr. Smith had been in September 1560, when Smith wrote to him in order to announce the jury's verdict, a few hours before he should have done. If it was suspicious for Robert to get to know Mr. Smith by letter, it has also been criticized that he "knew another juror personally".[4] The name of this supposed acquaintance was John Stevenson.

John Stevenson, from Southwell near Cumnor, had

---

1   Jackson 1878 p. 92
2   HMC Bath V p. 168; Adams 1995 p. 470; Jackson 1878 p. 92
3   Durning 2006 pp. 11, 13
4   Guy 2013 p. 189; Doran 2015 p. 124

possessions worth £9, according to the tax authorities. His brother Edward Stevenson also served as a juror (and, also from Southwell, was assessed with the equal amount).[1] Now, a John Steaphinson (or Stevenson) was also in Robert Dudley's service and it has been claimed that this man was the same as the juror.[2] Listed as a "ferrier" in a 1559 wages list between grooms of the stable and riders, his yearly salary was £4 and he lived in Robert's household, which cost Robert an extra £16 10s p. a. This John Stevenson also received a cap from Robert's haberdasher on one occasion.[3] Now, it appears that John Stevenson from Southwell near Cumnor came from a rather different social background than John Steaphinson the groom, and that John Stevenson the juror was not the servant in Robert Dudley's household. I therefore believe that there were two John Stevensons.

*

Four months after Amy died, Sir Henry Sidney had a chat with the Spanish ambassador. De Quadra was always very interested in the case of Lord Robert's wife, even though at the moment he had no Habsburg marriage candidate for Elizabeth on offer. Henry Sidney explained Robert's dilemma to the diplomatic bishop, who then reported the talk to King Philip:

> As regards the death of the wife, he was certain that it was accidental, and he had never been able to learn otherwise, although he had inquired with great care and knew that public opinion held to the contrary. I told him if what he said were true the evil was less, for, if murder had been

---

1 Skidmore 2010 p. 210
2 Skidmore 2010 p. 369
3 Adams 1995 pp. 414, 422

committed, God would never help nor fail to punish so abominable a crime, whatever men might do to mend it but that it would be difficult for Lord Robert to make things appear as he represented them. He answered it was quite true that no one believed it, and that even preachers in the pulpits discoursed on the matter in a way that was prejudicial to the honour and interests of the Queen.[1]

Henry Sidney made no bones about the fact that he was talking to de Quadra in order to support Robert's efforts to gain the queen's hand. It has accordingly been suggested that Sidney was not interested in the truth about Amy's death, and that therefore what he said to the ambassador has no significance for the question of how she died. It has also been suggested that he was simply too close to the Dudleys to be taken seriously as a witness.[2] However, Henry Sidney was also a man of an independent mind, as not only his career as Deputy of Ireland shows but also his memoirs, in which he openly described how the young Edward VI (who died in his arms) chose Jane Grey as his successor according to his own wish.[3] – This was not at all what official historiographers would have written in the 1580s, yet Sidney wrote down what he remembered to be the truth.

Henry Sidney was not only Mary Dudley's husband but also an expert on Spain and the Spanish language; he had travelled to the peninsula in 1554, he said with the purpose to speak for his imprisoned brothers-in-law at Philip's court.[4] He was successful in his mission and remained close to his brother-in-law Robert who in his turn played a significant

---

1 CSP Simancas I pp. 178–179
2 Skidmore 2010 p. 316
3 Literary Remains I p. ccliv
4 Adams 2002 p. 133

role in the life of Philip Sidney. The Sidneys being away in Ireland, Robert apparently grew fond of his little nephew (who had been left behind): Philip was about six when he received a crimson velvet cap with a silver hatband and feather from his uncle.[1] Henry Sidney's testimony regarding Amy Dudley's death should not be easily dismissed; yes, he was close to Robert Dudley and his interest, but he had also known his wife, something the authors of the *Journal* or *Leicester's Commonwealth* clearly had not.

*

We left Nicholas Throckmorton in the autumn of 1560, busily writing letters and sending messengers to the English court to warn Elizabeth about the consequences of marrying her beloved Robert. Back from his post as Elizabeth's ambassador to the King of France, he was next sent to Scotland where his task was to dissuade the Queen of Scots from a marriage with Lord Darnley (and encourage her to wed the Earl of Leicester instead). Throckmorton did what he could; he had long given up his resistance against the Dudley-Elizabeth marriage project, anyway, and had thereby become Robert Dudley's chief political advisor.[2] As it happened, he died in the latter's house on 12 February 1571. Of course *Leicester's Commonwealth* claimed that Robert had poisoned him with salads; Throckmorton had been suffering from tuberculosis for a long time, however, and his death was described as "a peripneumonia" by his doctors.[3] Robert described his death to Francis Walsingham, one of Throckmorton's successors at the Paris embassy:

> We have lost on Monday our good friend Sir

---
1 Adams 1995 p. 173
2 Adams 2002 p. 152
3 Lehmberg 2008

Nicholas Throckmorton, who died in my house, being there taken suddenly in great extremity on Tuesday before; his lungs were perished, but a sudden cold he had taken was the cause of his sudden death. God hath his soul, and we his friends great loss of his body.[1]

*

William Cecil sabotaged Robert Dudley's suit for the queen's hand from the moment Robert was a widower. Yet there is no reason to believe that he ever thought him to be guilty of his wife's death. We have seen how, shortly after the tragedy, he visited Robert at Kew to assure him of his friendship, apparently with success. It is hard to believe that he could have done this if he really believed Robert was guilty.

Later, in about 1565, Cecil wrote in an *aide-mémoire* that Robert was "infamed by the deth of his wiff" and that he was "hated of many; his wife's death".[2] These observations have been eagerly cited by some; however the odd nature of the document in which they appear is sometimes overlooked: This memorandum listed every conceivable defect of the Earl of Leicester as royal consort alongside every supposed advantage of the Archduke Charles in the same role. Thus, under "In likelihood to love his wife", Cecil wrote about Charles of Austria: "His father, Ferdinando, *ut supra*", meaning that Charles' father, the Emperor Ferdinand, had loved his wife very much. – He could not write anything about the archduke himself, as Charles had never been married so far. Turning to Robert, Cecil noted: "*Nuptiae carnales a laetitia incipiunt et in luctu terminantur.* Hated of many. His wife's death."[3]

---

1 Lehmberg 2008
2 Adams 2002 p. 140; Haynes p. 444
3 Wilson 1981 pp. 188–190

This was not a friendly remark, but in a sense it was just a statement of fact. Cecil wanted to remind himself to remind Elizabeth that marriages of love were to be avoided at all cost. Robert's marriage was just another example, having started in bliss or happiness (*laetitia*) and having ended in grief, sorrow, or mourning (*luctu[s]*).[1] Cecil, for his part, continued his intrigues against Robert's cause, both at home and abroad, for example by writing confidential letters to English diplomats. In 1566 he instructed Sir Thomas Hoby, Elizabeth's ambassador in Paris, to start a smear campaign in France against the Earl of Leicester, with the aim to make him unacceptable to Elizabeth.[2]

*

Cecil himself has been suggested as a possible suspect in Amy's death in recent decades, the first time in 1998 by the best-selling author Alison Weir:

> One man did profit from the death of Amy Dudley, and that was William Cecil. ... He was a perceptive man, and he could foresee that if she died in suspicious circumstances, as many people expected her to do, then the finger of suspicion would point inexorably to her husband – as indeed it did. Cecil also knew that Elizabeth ... would be unlikely to risk her popularity and her crown to marry a man whose reputation was so tainted.

---

1 Dr. Simon Adams translates *luctu* as "weeping" (Adams 2011). Antonia Fraser, unfortunately, in her classic biography of Mary Queen of Scots has given this phrase a sinister meaning, translating the sentence as "Carnal marriages begin with happiness and end in strife" (Fraser 1972 p. 274). This is not what the Latin words are saying.
2 Laoutaris 2014 pp. 79–80

In September 1560, Cecil had seen Dudley in the ascendant and his own future in ruins; he feared not only for his position, ... but also for the future of England and the Anglican Settlement.[1]

If Amy Dudley was murdered, Cecil is an excellent candidate according to the principle of *Cui bono?*. But did he have motive and opportunity? The founder of the Elizabethan secret service, Cecil would have been rightly placed to arrange the crime and to manipulate the coroner's jury afterwards (and we know that he did so in at least one case). What about his motive? As long as Amy Dudley lived her husband could not marry the queen, but what if she suffered from a serious illness? The evidence for this is inconclusive; yet unlike we, William Cecil would have known the truth. In case she was dying, Cecil would have had a strong motive indeed. Arguably, he was also the only person in a position to cover up the deed and obfuscate the facts in the long term.

*

In spring 1566, Amy's half-brother John Appleyard was staying with his brother-in-law William Huggyns at Hampton Court when he was approached by a mysterious man. This man promised him £1,000 if he would "be content to stir some matter against" the earl of Leicester, "for the death of his wife". Appleyard resisted the offer, declaring that "my Lord of Leicester is better my good lord than he is reported to be." And that "I will neither for gold or friend stand against him, but am and will be his to death". The mysterious man did not insist and "went away." Being asked later why he let the man go, Appleyard said that "he went over but in his night gown, and had no weapon about him, and that the other

---

[1] Weir 2008 p. 108

party had a servant standing not far off." – "Shutting the door" and making clear that "if I would be a villain to my Lord I could have money and friends great and good", he reported this adventure to Thomas Blount, saying he "thought little of it."[1]

Thomas Blount thought differently and told Leicester, who sent Blount to summon Appleyard to his presence. Appleyard did not show up as promised, though:

> Hearing no more, after some days the Earl sent to Blount from Greenwich, where the Court lay, to bring Appleyard to him, which he did. My Lord Marquis was then with Leicester. (The Marquis said that he remembered this.) Within a few words the Earl became so angry with Appleyard that it seemed that, if they had been alone, he would have drawn his sword upon him. He bade him depart and to Blount said that he was a very villain.[2]

This outburst of temper has been quoted in support of the theory that Robert had something to hide regarding the case of his wife; it is important to note, though, that William Parr, Marquess of Northampton, watched the scene. It is true that Northampton had been friendly with Leicester in the past, and that Leicester was in the marquess' company when he had Appleyard brought before him only reinforces this impression of friendship. If, however, Robert would have shared sinister secrets with Appleyard, or feared that Appleyard could compromise him, he would have met him in the company of a servant like Blount but not of an experienced courtier and intriguer like the marquess.

Appleyard was under the impression that the man who had

---

1 HMC Salisbury I p. 350; HMC Pepys p. 112
2 HMC Pepys p. 112

talked to him was acting on behalf of two noblemen, the Duke of Norfolk and the Earl of Sussex. Thomas Howard, 4th Duke of Norfolk, was the grandson of the man who had condemned Robert Dudley's father, and he resented the influence Robert had gained in Norfolk through his marriage and at court through his very special relationship with Elizabeth. The first peer of the realm, the Duke of Norfolk always believed he should be the only grandee about the queen. Though the Earl of Sussex had once been in favour of Elizabeth's marriage to Robert Dudley, their relationship had soured when Robert had unfairly criticized Sussex' policies in Ireland and sided with his enemies there.[1] It was certainly no coincidence that at this time these two aristocrats were also the chief promoters of Elizabeth's marriage with the Archduke Charles, a nearly lost cause by then for which they also blamed the Earl of Leicester.[2]

About a year after Leicester's row with Appleyard the privy council got wind that such illustrious persons as the Duke of Norfolk and the Earl of Sussex had been mentioned in connection with such murky transactions, and Appleyard was put in the Fleet prison. It was time for a major investigation. On the board sat William Cecil, as well as the Earl of Arundel, the Marquess of Northampton, Lord Admiral Clinton, and the Earl of Pembroke.[3]

We remember that Appleyard had been present at the inquest of 1560, and for several years he apparently had had no problem accepting the verdict. At some point however he began to think that the Earl of Leicester had not done enough for him, although in fact he had received many posts and advantages through his brother-in-law, like the office of Sheriff of Norfolk and Suffolk in 1559.[4] Nevertheless, he

---

1 Whitelock 2013 p. 47; MacCaffrey 2008
2 Hume 1904 p. 110
3 HMC Salisbury I p. 350
4 HMC Salisbury I p. 350; Williams 1964 p. 180

complained "that he had received many fair promises of good terms, but he never had the fruits thereof, although he had in the time of the Earl's trouble, which he specified to be in Queen Mary's time, ventured all that he had to help the said Earl and his wife."[1]

Appleyard appeared before the council in late May 1567, and it was noted that "[h]e denieth that ever he made any report or mention of the duke of Norfolk or earl of Sussex".[2] Cecil wrote down what else Appleyard had to say:

> [H]e said that he had oftentimes moved the Earl to give him leave and to countenance him in the prosecuting of the trial of the murder of his sister, adding that he did take the Earl to be innocent thereof, but yet he thought it an easy matter to find out the offenders, showing certain circumstances which moved him to think surely that she was murdered, whereunto the Earl always answered him that he thought it not fit to deal any further in the matter, considering that by order of law it was already found otherwise, and that it was so presented by a jury.

Appleyard said to this that "the jury had not as yet given up their verdict", as he thought. He also declared "that the Earl's displeasure towards him had been caused by Horsey and Christmas," two senior servants of Robert Dudley, but that "the Earl of his own disposition was his good lord."[3] In his anger, though, he was reported to have said quite differently, for Cecil noted on the back of that paper:

> Item, Tryndell saith that bringing answer from the

---

1 HMC Salisbury I p. 350
2 Skidmore 2010 p. 303
3 HMC Salisbury I p. 350

Earl of Leicester to Appleyard, that he could not help him in his requests, as he desired, Appleyard used words of anger, and said amongst other things, that he had for the Earl's sake covered the murder of his sister.[1]

We do not know who Tryndall was, except that he was probably Appleyard's servant. He overheard "John Appleyard and William Huggyns of Hampton Court reasoning together concerning the producing forth of a person that should declare such matter as partly is touched afore to be spoken to Appleyard," which means he heard them speak about the person who had offered £1,000 for the "stirring" of "some matter against" the Earl of Leicester regarding his wife's death. Tryndall had also heard Appleyard say to Huggyns "that he was sworn not to name the party, but he would point him out with his finger in the street," and that this "communication" between Appleyard and Huggyns occurred after Appleyard wrote a long letter to the Earl of Leicester.[2]

The council informed Appleyard that they would assist him in the examination of all the suspects that "he shall name, giving reasonable cause why he presents them"; he concluded that he desired a copy of the "coroner's verdict", and asked permission (after reading the verdict) "to take counsel's advice how to begin the trial of the cause."[3]

Appleyard, still in prison, received his copy of the coroner's report and then was charged to again explain himself in writing:

> The Lords would have you answer to these articles in writing with your own hand. First how and wherefore you devised the tales that were

---
1 HMC Salisbury I p. 351
2 HMC Salisbury I p. 351
3 HMC Salisbury I pp. 345–346

reported from you to my L. of Leicester, of certain persons that should solicit you in the name of my L. of Norfolk's grace, the Earl of Sussex and others, to stir up matter against my L. of Leicester for the death of his wife, for departure of the L. Darnley, and the stay of the Queen's Majesty's marriage, and therein to disclose the intention of your device from the beginning to the ending.

Secondly to declare plainly what moved you to use any speeches to cause the death of the Earl of Leicester's wife to be taken as procured by any person; and what you think thereof by the sight of the presentment made by the jury charged by the coroner and now returned into the King's Bench. To these matters the Lords would have you answer as plainly in writing at length as you have already done by speech.[1]

Apart from Appleyard, there were summoned a number of Robert Dudley's other men – among them Thomas Blount and William Huggyns, brother-in-law of John Appleyard, Keeper of the Gardens at Hampton Court, and former servant of the Duke and Duchess of Northumberland.[2] A man who interestingly was not summoned was Sir Richard Verney; it is possible that he was too ill, for he seems to have died in early 1568 (he may even have been dead already). He apparently was never mentioned in the proceedings.

In early May, just about the time the council initiated its investigation into Amy's death, Leicester had retired to Norfolk. He was sulking after some displeasure between him

---
1 HMC Salisbury XIII pp. 85–86
2 Adams 1995 p. 476. This William Huggyns / Huggon / Hogan is not to be confused with Amy Dudley's servant of the same name.

and the queen, though it is as likely that he wanted to be absent while the matter of his wife's death was in the air. We are not surprised that it was Thomas Blount and Nicholas Throckmorton who kept him informed:

> By Mr. Blunt's writing, you shall understand what hath been proceeding touching Appleyard. Huggon is sent for, after whose examination I think the matter shall suspend until you return. Lord Arundel remains here about that business. Lord Pembroke has shewed himself in this and in the handling of it your assured friend. Your well-willers would have you go through now with this matter.[1]

Cecil, meanwhile, wrote down the questions to be answered by Huggon / Huggyns:

> How often did John Appleyard inform you of any offers made to him to provoke him to prosecute matter against my lord of Leicester? Where were you when Appleyard went over the Thames to speak with one that came to move him in such a purpose? Who came to fetch Appleyard? How many persons did you see on the other side of the Thames with Appleyard? Did Appleyard stand or walk whilst he communed with the party?[2]

Cecil prepared even more questions for other people he unfortunately did not name, but one question was: "What talk have you had with the Duke of Norfolk, the Earl of Sussex, and the Earl of Leicester within the last three years?" Another was: "What occasion moveth you to haunt so familiarly the

---
1 HMC Pepys p. 103
2 HMC Salisbury I pp. 351–352

company of Tryndell?" Respecting Tryndall, Cecil wrote down for a second time what the former had said about Appleyard, Huggyns, and Amy Dudley:

> Trendle. That he heard Huggyns and him reason about discovery that he had sworn not name; that he in anger said that he had covered the death of his wife.[1]

On 4 June, after "a full month" of imprisonment, Appleyard, "afflicted with sickness and most miserable poverty, not having money left to find himself two meals", broke down. Having read the coroner's verdict, which he had returned the previous day, he changed his mind and declared that in

> which verdict I do find, not only such proofs testified under the oaths of fifteen persons, how my late sister by misfortune happened to death, but also such manifest and plain demonstration thereof, as has fully and clearly satisfied and persuaded me; and therefore, my lords, commending her soul to God, I have not further to say of that cause. For I have of your honours required nothing that might bring trial of her unhappy case to light, but I have in all justice received the same, yea, even with the offer of your noble assistances.[2]

Appleyard was released, but had to appear before Star Chamber where he said that "he [had] accused my Lord of Leicester only for malice",[3] having already asked the two

---

1 HMC Salisbury I p. 351. See also above p. 124.
2 Skidmore 2010 p. 305
3 Skidmore 2010 p. 305

"noble gentlemen against whom he has trespassed" – Norfolk and Sussex – for pardon.[1]

*

Appleyard's brushes with the authorities were not over yet. In the aftermath of the Northern Rebellion, in early 1570, he led his own local rebellion in Norfolk – he even hoped to betray the port of Yarmouth to the Spanish Duke of Alba.[2] At the time more than 750 rebels were executed in England, but Appleyard escaped execution, receiving life imprisonment. In his trial he maintained that he was "to have had [his co-conspirators] to a banquet, and to have betrayed them all, and to have won credit thereby with the Queen", however this was hardly the reason he escaped the death penalty. It seems obvious that his excellent court connections played a major role in his survival. They certainly did when four years later, his health failing, Appleyard was transferred from Norwich castle to the more comfortable quarters in the Dean of Norwich' house, by royal order. The Dean of Norwich happened to be a good friend and protégé of the Earl of Leicester.[3]

The case of John Appleyard is certainly mysterious. Imprisoned, he was under pressure from the council; yet the council also questioned several of Leicester's servants and it appears that an honest inquiry would have been possible if Appleyard had really supplied names. It would seem that he had nothing substantial to reveal.

Appleyard died at the dean's house at some unknown date after 31 May 1574.[4] His son Henry was in Leicester's service in the 1570s and was trusted with carrying his lordship's

---

1 HMC Salisbury I p. 346
2 Williams 1964 pp. 180–182
3 Williams 1964 pp. 182, 186, 188, 174; Wilson 1981 p. 183
4 Wilson 1981 p. 183

dispatches from the Netherlands in 1586, when Leicester served there as governor-general.[1] If Appleyard really had known interesting details about his half-sister's death the question arises why Robert Dudley would not have found means to remove him from the scene entirely? The 1570 rebellion would have been the perfect opportunity.

The same goes for William Cecil, who as we saw led the whole inquiry of 1567. We will never know whether he became nervous as Appleyard opened his mouth; but in a letter to Leicester he informed him of what he thought of Appleyard and his ilk: "If William Huggyns be with your Lordship, I pray you let him come with your Lordship that he may be spoken withal upon the sudden, concerning Appleyard, for amongst them they will fall out in their own colours."[2] – We can be sure that if Appleyard had known the killer of Amy Dudley by name, as he had claimed, Cecil, if not Leicester, would have found a way to dispatch this dangerous man once and for all.

William Cecil had his enemies, and some have counted Robert Dudley among them. Would he, could he have lived for decades knowing what Cecil had done to his wife – and his reputation – if, *if* Cecil had been behind Amy's death? On one occasion, in September 1578, Robert wrote to Cecil complaining about some misunderstanding concerning the Mint and even hinting at some obscure wrong done to him in the past. Murder, though, apparently was not on his mind, while there was hope for renewed friendship:

> We began our service with our sovereign together and have long continued hitherto together. And touching your fortune I am sure yourself cannot have a thought that ever I was enemy to it. ... What opinion you have indeed of me, I have ...

---

1   Adams 1995 p. 362
2   HMC Pepys p. 119

somewhat in doubt, though I promise you I know no cause in the world in myself that I have given you other than good. You may suppose this to be a strange humour in me to write thus and in this sort to you, having never done the like before, although I must confess I have had more cause of unkindness (as I have thought) than by this trifling occasion.

Your Lordship is more acquainted by years with the world than I am. And yet, by reason we live in a worse world where more cunning and less fidelity is used, may judge of bad and good dealing as well as an elder man, and the one being so common and the other so scant must make the proof of the better the more precious whenever it is found. And surely, my Lord, where I profess, I will be found both a faithful and a just, honest friend.[1]

*

Thomas Blount died in 1568. Blount had been a cousin of the Duchess of Northumberland, Robert's mother, and had served the Duke of Northumberland as comptroller of the household in the early 1550s. After his master's downfall he entered the service of Robert Dudley, even before Elizabeth's accession, and became his "principal administrative officer".[2] If one man ever found out what happened to Amy it was him.

Anthony Forster died in 1572. Another lifelong servant of Robert Dudley and his father, he had been busy buying tapestries for Kenilworth Castle as late as July 1572.[3] From

---

1 TNA SP XII/125/73
2 Adams 1995 p. 464
3 Wilson 1981 pp. 149–150. Elizabeth had granted Kenilworth to Robert

1566 he had also been MP for Abingdon. He was buried in the parish church at Cumnor next to his house – for he had bought Cumnor Place from Dr. Owen's son, William, the year after Amy's death. A Latin epitaph celebrated his talents as a musician, gardener, and builder:

> He knew how to stretch skilfully the sounding chord of the muses and to strike the a[e]onian lyre. He rejoiced to settle young plants in the earth and with remarkable skill to build noble houses.[1]

Cumnor Place he bequeathed to Robert Dudley, who sold it in 1574 to Henry Norris. Norris's wife Margery had acted as chief mourner at Amy's funeral and she interestingly was the cousin of Anthony Forster's wife.[2] Henry Norris and his wife remained good friends with Robert Dudley, who regularly visited them, with and without the queen, at Rycote, Oxfordshire. It was here that he wrote the last letter of his life on 29 August 1588.

*

Almost to the day 28 years after Amy had been found dead at Cumnor Place, Robert Dudley died only a few miles away. He spent his last days in illness at Cornbury Park, a hunting lodge he was entitled to use in connection with one of his offices. England was now at war with Spain – having just prevailed over the *Grande y Felicísima Armada* – and the last Spanish ambassador had left in 1584. King Philip had thus to rely on spies; one of them, the Genoese merchant Marco Antonio Messia, reported:

Dudley in 1563.
1 Harding 1981
2 Harding 1981

> On the 27th [of August] the earl of Leicester started for the baths of Buxton, but on the way, in the house of a gentleman near Oxford, it is said he supped heavily, and being troubled with distress in the stomach during the night he forced himself to vomit. This brought on a tertian fever, which increased to such an extent on the third day that on Wednesday, 4th [September], at ten o'clock in the morning, he expired. The last time I saw him was at the earl of Essex's review, at the window with the Queen.[1]

Ten days later another spy sent an update of court gossip:

> Leicester died almost suddenly on his way to the baths, and in the same house as that in which he had caused his wife to be killed, the master of it having invited him to dinner. The Queen is sorry for his death, but no other person in the country. She was so grieved that for some days she shut herself in her chamber alone, and refused to speak to anyone until the Treasurer and other Councillors had the doors broken open and entered to see her.[2]

Sweet Robin (as she had called him) lived on in Elizabeth's heart and never died, and other than after Amy's death the court never went into official mourning for Robert Dudley.

His funeral cost about £3,000, just a thousand pounds more than his first wife's. His second wife, Lettice, whom he had secretly married in 1578, attended the ceremony, however none of the senior privy councillors seem to have put in an appearance. Christopher Hatton, Lord Chancellor,

---
1 CSP Simancas IV pp. 420–421
2 CSP Simancas IV p. 431

and Francis Walsingham, Principal Secretary, had wanted to go but then had changed their minds, though both had been Leicester's friends. Was it politic to stay away from the widowed Countess of Leicester – *persona non grata* at Elizabeth's court, not unlike Amy Dudley before her?

Meanwhile, Sir Henry Killigrew wanted to pay his respects. He had served Leicester's father before becoming a diplomat and servant of the queen, and the closeness to his old patrons always remained. He asked the privy council for permission to leave his post in the Netherlands, "that I may yield him the last service and testimony of my devotion at his funerals."[1] His request was rejected.

Amy Dudley's illegitimate half-brother, Arthur Robsart, also would have liked to attend Robert Dudley's funeral. In 1560 he had attended Amy's funeral at Robert's invitation. This time, alas, there was no-one to invite him, yet he remembered his brother-in-law as "my cheife frend gone, the yerle of Lesseter".[2]

---

1 Adams 1995 p. 349
2 Adams 1995 p. 483

NINE

EPILOGUE

Long before Robert Dudley's death, his first wife's "murder" had become part of Elizabethan political folklore, together with other would-be scandals. An early Spanish report said that Amy "was found in a country house with a stroke from the point of a dagger in her head"[1] – perhaps an allusion to her head injuries – while a mid-1580s report from Robert Dudley's Catholic enemies really got a lot of things mixed up: According to these people the Earl of Leicester had "allured into treason" the earls of Northumberland and Westmoreland (two Catholic northern magnates who had as good as never appeared at court and rebelled against Elizabeth in 1569), and now,

> none being left to control him, he lifted up his head, insinuated himself into the Queen's favour, and got the highest offices; married a lady of noble birth, but plotted with Dame Lettice, his mistress, to make away with both her husband and his wife. So as the lady was in the country, playing with her ladies at table, she left the room, fell down stairs, and broke her neck, being thrown down by order of her lord; but he gave it out it was by chance, and no one durst say the contrary. He next procured the murder by poison

---

1   González p. 69

of the Earl of Essex, ... pretending he was ill of an incurable disease, and all sorts of potions were sent to cure him, but without effect. ... Dame Lettice put on black, to veil her content, and though there was much whispering, no man durst speak, he was so grown in Her Majesty's favour.[1]

In this story Robert kills his wife *because he wants to marry Lettice*, Countess of Essex. The wife that is pushed down the stairs seems to be a blend of Douglas Sheffield (who indeed was of noble birth but who almost certainly never married him) and Amy. He then has Lettice's husband, Walter Devereux, 1st Earl of Essex, poisoned, although Walter was away in Ireland. There the real Walter had died in 1576, of dysentery, "a mere flux, a disease appropriate to this country and whereof there died many", as Lord Deputy Henry Sidney concluded in his report about the death.[2]

*

Robert Dudley, from the early days of his life as the queen's favourite, was very much a celebrity, and all manner of rumours circulated about him and Elizabeth – at all levels of society, from disaffected aristocrats to foreign merchants and ambassadors, from provincial gentlemen (and -women) to peasants. The majority of these stories revolved around the "fact" that the queen had children by Lord Robert, but, as we have seen, some were concerned with the nature of his wife's death. Contemporaries apparently did not take such rumours particularly seriously, and understandably historians and biographers do not believe the stories about secret children. Oddly, they have been slightly more inclined to believe in Amy's murder.

---

1 CSP Dom XII pp. 136–137
2 Freedman 1983 p. 33–34

If Amy Dudley was murdered a couple of larger questions arise that do not present themselves with the alternatives of accident and suicide: Why did Robert Dudley's fellow courtier-statesmen apparently believe him innocent of his wife's death? Why did his enemies, people of very high social standing, never succeed in destroying him? Why did people who would have known of the deed, or even committed it themselves, die natural deaths decades later? One could argue that as the queen's favourite the Earl of Leicester was untouchable. But is this true? Would Queen Elizabeth have perverted justice to such a degree as to condone a murder which affected her honour so deeply? Did she stick to her motto, *Video et Taceo*, "I see and keep silent"? But then how could she have continued to love – and trust – the man she once described as "another ourself"?[1]

That Robert would have been stupid enough to orchestrate his wife's death in a manner that laid him open to a foreseeable scandal has been judged as highly unlikely. After all, Amy's death such as it occurred diminished any chances he had to marry the queen, be it through divorce or a less controversial death.[2]

How long could Robert Dudley have survived, physically and politically, if he had been guilty of his wife's murder? Would he have risked the axe for murder, having narrowly escaped it for treason a few years before? It may seem an odd observation in the face of a Tudor king who executed two of his wives, but Amy's murder would arguably have been the only case of high society wife-killing in England during the entire 16th century.[3]

Not so in Italy. The famous composer of madrigals,

---

[1] Lovell 2006 p. 265. In a letter to the Earl of Shrewsbury, 25 June 1577.
[2] Pollard 1910 p. 239; Weir 2008 p. 107; Wilson 2005 p. 275
[3] There were slightly more cases of high-born wives killing their husbands; Agnes Lady Hungerford was hanged in 1523 (after the death of her second husband, Sir Edward Hungerford) for the murder of her first husband, James Cotell (Bellamy 2005 pp. 129–130).

Gesualdo, killed his unfaithful wife with her lover, in the act, but then he was a prince and thus his own lord. There were also Isabella de' Medici and her cousin Leonora di Garzia di Toledo: Both princesses were strangled by their respective husbands in isolated country villas within five days in July 1576. Dying from very odd "accidents" – Leonora had suffocated in bed, Isabella had "fallen dead" while "washing her hair in the morning"[1] – no commentator had any doubts about the true nature of the young women's demises (which had even been witnessed by servants), and the crimes have often been seen as punishment for the ladies' interesting love life. Notwithstanding the latter, the murders were in all likelihood committed on the orders of the Grand Duke of Tuscany, Francesco I, Isabella's brother. The grand duke's only problem was how to explain the sudden deaths to King Philip II, as both women were Spanish aristocrats by descent.[2]

The French special envoy to Elizabeth's court, Simier, who brought his master's – *Monsieur's* – love tokens to England in 1579, also had his wife (and his brother) killed in a fit of jealousy the year before and he was obviously allowed to go free.[3] However, the mentality of Italy, Spain, and other countries of the Mediterranean was rather different from that of Northern Europe, England included, where the treatment of wives was concerned.

*

In the 1570s, Edward de Vere, 17th Earl of Oxford, a man with a big grudge against the Earl of Leicester, apparently too wanted to capitalize from the strange death of Amy Dudley in some way: The details are totally obscure, though, Oxford's

---

1 Murphy 2008 p. 324
2 Murphy 2008 pp. 316–333
3 Hume 1904 p. 199

intrigues surviving only in garbled reports of what he was supposed to have said to a variety of people later hostile to him. What is clear is that his efforts to discredit the Earl of Leicester by raking up old stories were in vain. He next planned physical attacks and used graffiti.[1] It was those erstwhile friends of Edward de Vere who were also behind *Leicester's Commonwealth*. This anti-Leicester book was composed in France in 1583 or so and smuggled into England in the spring of 1584. It was immediately suppressed by the government and therefore survives mostly in manuscript copies. Nevertheless, it circulated widely and was reprinted in 1641, having an enormous influence on later writers. It was thus guaranteed that its version of Amy's "murder" survived, including the often-repeated detail about the undisturbed "hood that stood upon her head" as she was found.

As early as 1608 *A Yorkshire Tragedy*, a so-called domestic tragedy (a genre featuring domestic dramas) alluded to Amy's fall as an easy way to get rid of one's talkative wife:

> Down stairs,
> Tumble, tumble, headlong. So –
> The surest way to charm a woman's tongue
> Is, break her neck. A politician did it."[2]

John Webster's revenge tragedy, *The White Devil* (1612), likewise alludes to Leicester's crimes, allocating them to Paolo Giordano Orsini, Duke of Bracciano and fellow wife murderer:[3]

> You that were held the famous politician;

---

1 Nelson 2003 p. 201
2 Chamberlin 1939 pp. 417–418
3 Paolo Giordano Orsini was Isabella de' Medici's husband.

> Whose art was poison.
> And whose conscience murder.
> That would have broke your wife's neck down the stairs
> Ere she was poisoned[1]

Next there is a reference to "your villainous sallets", a hint that Webster may have read *Leicester's Commonwealth* where Throckmorton is poisoned eating Leicester's salad.[2] Attached to some of the 1641 copies of *Leicester's Commonwealth* was a poem, *Leicester's Ghost*. Here, Leicester speaks in the first person:

> My wife first fell downe from a paire of staires
> And broke her neck and so at Cumnor died,
> Whilst her true servants led with small affaires
> Unto a faire at Abbington did ride
> This dismal hap unto my wife betide
>
> Whether yee call it charm or destinie
> Too true it is shee did untimely die.
>
> O had I now a showre of teares to shed
> Lockt in the empty circles of mine eyes,
> Or could I shed in mourning for the dead
> That lost a spouse so young, so faire, so wise,
> So faire a corps, so foul a corse now lies;
>
> My hope to have married with a famous Queene
> Drove pitty back and kept my teares unseene.[3]

It was the 19th century that truly immortalized Amy. In 1821

---

1 Webster, *The White Devil*, V, 3
2 Peck 1985 pp. 60, 131; Webster, *The White Devil*, V, 3
3 Pettigrew 1859 p. 11

Walter Scott's historical novel *Kenilworth* was published, triggering a Romantic fascination with her. Amy Robsart, under her maiden name, became the meek, innocent, illiterate (yes, it was claimed that she could not write[1]) murder victim. An immediate bestseller, *Kenilworth* engendered many other works of art: A play by Victor Hugo, two operas – by Auber (1823) and Donizetti (1829) – as well as countless paintings. Among the most gifted artists who painted the doomed Amy (with and without her husband) were Richard Parkes Bonington, Edward Matthew Ward, and William Frederick Yeames.

We are not really surprised to learn that the novel's arch-villain is called Varney. This ruffian-servant of Robert kills Amy (Amelia in the operas), against his master's orders. Amy herself is the secret Countess of Leicester, Elizabeth having no idea that Robert is married. Scott merged at least two of Robert Dudley's "wives" in the character of Amy Robsart, the real Amy and Douglas Sheffield, Robert's 1570s mistress, who many years later claimed to have married him in secret. The story is set in 1575, culminating in the legendary Kenilworth festival where Leicester entertained Queen Elizabeth for 19 days. The novel thus freely mixes up personas and chronology. It nevertheless had a huge impact on 19th century scholars, who now endeavoured to investigate the murder case of Amy Robsart.

Several English historians travelled to Simancas to view the archives of the Spanish kings. The Catholic historian John Lingard found de Feria's dispatch which reported that Lord Robert's wife was afflicted, in Lingard's words, "with a painful complaint in her chest" and that it was "openly said" that Robert "waited only for her death in order to accomplish his marriage with the queen".[2] James Anthony Froude also

---

1 Adlard 1870 p. 22
2 Chamberlin 1939 p. 425

read de Feria's letter at Simancas, translating the interesting passage as "a cancer on the breast".[1] Froude adored Henry VIII and held no high opinion of either Anne Boleyn or Elizabeth, and especially not of Robert Dudley.[2] His findings in de Quadra's dispatches, rumours of poison and divorce, did nothing to change this. Writing in 1863, he concluded about Amy and Robert:

> [A]lthough Dudley was innocent of a direct participation in the crime, the unhappy lady was sacrificed to his ambition. She was murdered by persons who hoped to profit by his elevation to the throne; and Dudley himself – aware that if murder could be proved, public feeling would forbid his marriage with the queen – used private means, notwithstanding his affectation of sincerity, to prevent the search from being pressed inconveniently far.[3]

Amy Robsart was also a favourite subject of 19th century antiquarians and local historians. Thomas Joseph Pettigrew, George Adlard, and Canon J. E. Jackson printed valuable documents and wrote in defence of Robert Dudley, Anthony Forster, and Richard Verney, while Walter Rye prepared *A Brief for the Prosecution*, drawing on poison charges and *Leicester's Commonwealth*.[4] By 1910, A. F. Pollard, a widely read professor, believed that the fact that Amy Robsart's death caused suspicion was "as natural as it was incredible ... But a meaner intelligence than Elizabeth's or even Dudley's

---

1 Froude 1911 p. 60
2 Froude 1911 p. 60; Chamberlin 1939 p. 23
3 Froude 1911 p. 202
4 Pettigrew 1859; Adlard 1870; Jackson 1878; Rye 1885

would have perceived that murder would make the marriage impossible."[1]

The 20th century became less obsessed with Amy's "murder", and most of Elizabeth's biographers inclined towards accident or suicide or, after 1956, an accident brought on by breast cancer as cause of death. This was the situation until about 2010 when the news of the discovery of the coroner's report hit the media. As we have seen, the report not only says that Amy died from a broken neck after falling "to the bottom" of certain steps, but also that she incurred two head wounds. The latter especially have attracted attention and were presented as an indication or even proof of murder, while the very same report's verdict of accident was strangely ignored. The updated 2011 entry in the *Oxford Dictionary of National Biography* concluded, though, that "[t]he head wounds add a new twist, but they are compatible with either accident or foul play."[2]

Meanwhile, as a side effect of the on-going search for an authentic portrait of Amy's sister-in-law, Lady Jane Grey, it was suggested that a portrait miniature might depict Amy Robsart as a bride. In 1983, the picture was dated to c.1550 by Sir Roy Strong, Director of the National Portrait Gallery, who believed it was commissioned from Levina Teerlinc by the 17-year-old Princess Elizabeth. The lady in the miniature "wears a gold brooch mounted with a black classical head and behind it a bunch of acorns and a spray of yellow flowers".[3] The inscription "AON XVIII" means either that the sitter is 18 years old or in her 18th year. Of course, Amy, on her wedding day in 1550, was only three days away from her 18th birthday and thus in her 17th year, or almost 18. The yellow flowers have been identified as gillyflowers or

---
1   Pollard 1910 pp. 238–239
2   Adams 2011
3   Ives 2009 p. 15

possibly cowslips,[1] gillyflowers serving as a general symbol of marriage and fidelity.[2] The flowers in the miniature are "impaled", that is arranged to symbolize "a marriage between a man whose badge was an oak and a woman whose badge was a flower."[3]

We know that Robert Dudley actually used the oak symbolism in his youth: One of the carvings in the Beauchamp Tower at the Tower of London has an oak tree and the initials R D, and the more elaborate Dudley carving made by his brother, John, Earl of Warwick, also uses acorns and oak leaves. The pun derived from the similarity of Robert's name to the Latin word for oak, *robur*.

There are thus some good arguments to identify the 1550 miniature as Amy Robsart. There have also been other theories: That it shows Elizabeth I as princess, Katherine Howard, Lady Jane Grey, or even Mary I as princess. However none of these suggestions explains why the lady should wear acorns around her jewel.

It must be asked of course: How common were such pictures? How many people would have commissioned such things? Also, if this is really a portrait of Amy, would that not point to Robert Dudley having kept it after her death? There survive many inventories of Robert's vast collections of paintings and beautiful artefacts, more than of any other Elizabethan nobleman, alas such a miniature seems not to be among the items listed and described.[4]

*

With the passage of time, Amy's grave in the chancel of St. Mary's Church, Oxford, was forgotten. Following a fire in

---

1   Ives 2009 pp. 15–16; Edwards 2007
2   Skidmore 2010 p. 21
3   Edwards 2007
4   Inventories are printed in Goldsmith 2014 pp. 255–311.

1946, excavations were undertaken in the chancel; it was found that further vaults had been built in the 18th and 19th centuries, and "that the whole floor area" had "been completely disturbed" at "sometime subsequent to the date of her death and burial."[1] Today, a small tile of marble can be found in the floor:

In a Vault of brick
At the upper end of this Quire
Was buried
AMY ROBSART
On Sunday 22nd September
A.D.1560

*

---

1 Skidmore 2010 pp. 375–376

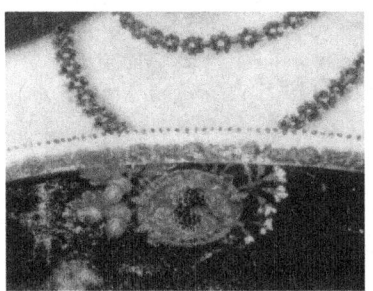

Figure 3: The Yale miniature's spray of flowers, acorns, and oak leaves around a gold brooch mounted with a black classical head. (See also Figure 1).

Bibliography

Primary sources

Acts of the Privy Council of England. http://www.british-history.ac.uk/search/series/acts-privy-council

Adams, Simon (ed.) **(1995)**: *Household Accounts and Disbursement Books of Robert Dudley, Earl of Leicester, 1558–1561, 1584–1586.* Cambridge University Press.

Adams, Simon; **Archer**, Ian; **Bernard**, G. W. (eds.) **(2003a)**: "Certayne Brife Notes of the Controversy betwene the dukes of Somerset and Nor[t]humberland" in: Ian Archer (ed.): *Religion, Politics, and Society in Sixteenth-Century England.* Cambridge University Press.

Adams, Simon; **Archer**, Ian; **Bernard**, G. W. (eds.) **(2003b)**: "A 'Journall' of Matters of State happened from time to time as well within and without the Realme from and before the Death of King Edw. the 6th untill the Yere 1562" in: Ian Archer (ed.): *Religion, Politics, and Society in Sixteenth-Century England.* Cambridge University Press.

Four pencil sketches containing a plan, with a doorway and details of part of the abbey at Abingdon; drawn by Samuel Lysons, Esq. **BL** Additional MS 9460 f.74.b.

The **Chronicle of Queen Jane** *and Two Years of Queen Mary.* (ed. J. G. Nichols, 1850). Camden Society.

Chronicle of the Greyfriars *of London.* (ed. J. G. Nicholls, 1852). Camden Society.

Collins, Arthur (ed.) **(1746)**: *Letters and Memorials of State I.* T. Osborne.

Calendar of State Papers, Domestic Series. Longmans.

Calendar of State Papers, Foreign. http://www.british-history.ac.uk/search/series/cal-state-papers--foreign

Calendar of ... State Papers Relating to English Affairs ... in ... Simancas, 1558–1603. (ed. Martin Hume, 1892–1899). HMSO.

Calendar of State Papers Relating to English Affairs in the Archives of Venice. http://www.british-history.ac.uk/search/series/cal-state-papers--venice

Durning, Louise (ed.) **(2006)**: *Queen Elizabeth's Book of Oxford.*

Bodleian Library.

González, Tomás: *Documents from Simancas Relating to the Reign of Elizabeth (1558–1568)*. (ed. Spencer Hall, 1865).

Hardwicke State Papers. (1778).

Haynes, Samuel (ed.) (1740): *A Collection of State Papers ... Left by William Cecill, Lord Burghley*. William Bowyer.

*Manuscripts of The Marquess of **Bath** Volume V: Talbot, Dudley and Devereux Papers 1533–1659* (ed. Historical Manuscript Commission, 1980). HMSO.

*Report on the **Pepys** Manuscripts Preserved at Magdalen College, Cambridge*. (ed. Historical Manuscript Commission, 1911).

*Calendar of the Manuscripts of ... The Marquess of **Salisbury** ... Preserved at Hatfield House, Hertfordshire*. (ed. Historical Manuscripts Commission). HMSO.

Second Report of the Royal Commission on Historical Manuscripts. (ed. 1874).

Holinshed, Raphael: *Chronicles of England, Scotland, and Ireland*. (1577). http://english.nsms.ox.ac.uk/holinshed/index.php

Relations politiques de Pays-Bas et de l'Angleterre sous règne de Philippe II. (ed. Kervyn de Lettenhove, 1882–1900).

Literary Remains of King Edward the Sixth. (ed. G. J. Nichols, 1857). Roxburghe Club.

The Diary of Henry Machyn. (ed. G. J. Nichols, 1848). Camden Society.

Peck, D. C. (ed.) (1985): *Leicester's Commonwealth: The Copy of a Letter Written by a Master of Art of Cambridge (1584) and Related Documents*. Ohio University Press.

Rodríguez-Salgado, M. J. and Adams, Simon (eds.) (1984): "The Count of Feria's Dispatch to Philip II of 14 November 1558". *Camden Miscellany*. Volume XXVIII. Royal Historical Society.

Coroner's Report into the death of Amy Robsart, August 1561. TNA KB 9/1073/f.80
http://www.nationalarchives.gov.uk/education/resources/elizabeth-monarchy/coroners-report/

Robert Dudley to William Cecil, September 1578. TNA SP XII/125/73

von Klarwill, Victor (ed.) (1928): *Queen Elizabeth and Some Foreigners*. John Lane.

Wright, Thomas (ed.) (1838): *Queen Elizabeth and Her Times*. Henry Colburn.

Secondary sources

Adams, Simon (2002): *Leicester and the Court: Essays in Elizabethan Politics*. Manchester University Press.

Adams, Simon (2008a): "Dudley, Ambrose, earl of Warwick (c.1530–1590)". *Oxford Dictionary of National Biography*. Online edition.

Adams, Simon (2008b): "Dudley, Robert, earl of Leicester (1532/3–1588)". *Oxford Dictionary of National Biography*. Online edition.

Adams, Simon (2011): "Dudley, Amy, Lady Dudley (1532–1560)". *Oxford Dictionary of National Biography*. Online edition.

Adlard, George (1870): *Amye Robsart and the Earl of Leycester*. John Russell Smith.

Aird, Ian (1956): "The Death of Amy Robsart". *The English Historical Review*. Vol. 71. No. 278. May 1956.

Baker, T. F. T. (1982): "BUTLER, Anthony (by 1522-70), of London; Rycote, Oxon. and Coates, nr. Stow, Lincs.". *The History of Parliament*. http://www.historyofparliamentonline.org/volume/1509-1558/member/butler-anthony-1522-70

Bakewell, Sarah (2004): "Bayley, Walter (1529–1593)". *Oxford Dictionary of National Biography*. Online edition.

Bellamy, John (2005): *Strange, Inhuman Deaths: Murder in Tudor England*. Sutton.

Bernard, George (2000): *Power and Politics in Tudor England*. Ashgate.

Bossy, John (2006): "Trust the Coroner". *London Review of Books*. Vol. 28, No. 24.

Chamberlin, Frederick (1939): *Elizabeth and Leycester*. Dodd, Mead & Co.

Doran, Susan (1996): *Monarchy and Matrimony: The Courtships of Elizabeth I*. Routledge.

Doran, Susan (2013): "Queen Elizabeth I of England: Monarchical Leadership in Action" in: Peter Ivar Kaufmann: *Leadership and Elizabethan Culture*. Palgrave Macmillan.

Doran, Susan (2015): *Elizabeth I and Her Circle*. Oxford University Press.

Edwards, J. S. (2007): "The Yale Miniature Portrait". http://www.somegreymatter.com/starkeyminiature.htm

Ehrlich, E. and H. Maxeiner (2002): "External injury marks (wounds) on the head in different types of blunt trauma in an autopsy series". *Medicine and Law*. 2002. 21(4):773-82. https://www.ncbi.nlm.nih.gov/pubmed/15796004

Elizabeth I: Killer Queen? http://www.natgeotv.com/uk/elizabeth-i-killer-queen
"Erdbeben im Urlaubsparadies". Frankfurter Rundschau 15.07.2008. http://www.fr.de/panorama/rhodos-erdbeben-im-urlaubsparadies-a-1178342
Ferrari et al. (2012): "Osteoporosis in young adults: pathophysiology, diagnosis, and management". *Osteoporosis International*. 2012 Dec;23(12):2735-48. https://www.ncbi.nlm.nih.gov/pubmed/22684497
Fraser, Antonia (1972): *Mary Queen of Scots*. Pan.
Fraser, Antonia (1996): *The Gun Powder Plot: Terror & Faith in 1605*. Weidenfeld & Nicolson.
Freedman, Sylvia (1983): *Poor Penelope: Lady Penelope Rich. An Elizabethan Woman*. The Kensal Press.
Frick, H.; Leonhardt, H.; Starck, D. (1991): *Human Anatomy I: General Anatomy. Special Anatomy I: Limbs, Trunk Wall, Head and Neck*. Thieme.
Froude, J. A. (1911): *The Reign of Elizabeth I*. Everyman's Library.
Goldring, Elizabeth (2014): *Robert Dudley, Earl of Leicester, and the World of Elizabethan Art*. Yale University Press.
Gristwood, Sarah (2007): *Elizabeth and Leicester: Power, Passion, Politics*. Viking.
Guy, John (2013): *The Children of Henry VIII*. Oxford University Press.
Guyomarc'h et al. (2010): "Discrimination of falls and blows in blunt head trauma: a multi-criteria approach". *Journal of Forensic Sciences*. 2010. Mar 1. 55(2):423-7. Epub 2010 Feb 5. http://www.ncbi.nlm.nih.gov/pubmed/20141554
Harding, Alan (1981): "FORSTER, Anthony (c.1510-72), of Cumnor Place, Berks. and Cripplegate, London". *The History of Parliament*. http://www.historyofparliamentonline.org/volume/1558-1603/member/forster-anthony-1510-72
Hartweg, Christine (2016): *John Dudley: The Life of Lady Jane Grey's Father-in-Law*. Createspace.
Haynes, Alan (1987): *The White Bear: The Elizabethan Earl of Leicester*. Peter Owen.
"HUBAND, John (c.1544-83), of Leominster, Herefs.; Hillbarrow, Ippsley and Temple Grafton, Warws." *The History of Parliament*. http://www.historyofparliamentonline.org/volume/1558-1603/member/huband-john-1544-83
Hume, Martin (1904): *The Courtships of Queen Elizabeth*. Eveleigh Nash & Grayson.

Inman, Peggy (n.d.): "Amy Robsart and Cumnor Place". http://www.bodley.ox.ac.uk/external/cumnor/articles/inman-robsart.htm
Ives, Eric (2009): *Lady Jane Grey: A Tudor Mystery*. Wiley-Blackwell.
Jackson, J. E. (1878): "Amye Robsart". *The Wiltshire Archaeological and Natural History Magazine*. Vol. XVII.
Jenkins, Elizabeth (1961): *Elizabeth and Leicester*. Victor Gollancz.
Jones, Norman (1993): *The Birth of the Elizabethan Age: England in the 1560s*. Blackwell.
"Junge (12) stirbt bei Schulausflug". Bild 02.04.2014. http://www.bild.de/regional/berlin/schueler/stirbt-auf-schulausflug-in-brandenburg-36522346.bild.html
Kremer et al. (2008): "Discrimination of falls and blows in blunt head trauma: systematic study of the hat brim line rule in relation to skull fractures". *Journal of Forensic Sciences*. 2008 May. 53(3):716-9. http://www.ncbi.nlm.nih.gov/pubmed/18471221
Kremer, C. and Sauvageau, A. (2009): "Discrimination of falls and blows in blunt head trauma: assessment of predictability through combined criteria". *Journal of Forensic Sciences*. 2009 Jul.54(4):923-6. https://www.ncbi.nlm.nih.gov/pubmed/19486249
Laoutaris, Chris (2014): *Shakespeare and the Countess: The Battle That Gave Birth to The Globe*. Fig Tree.
Lehmberg, Stanford (2008): "Throckmorton, Sir Nicholas (1515/16–1571)". *Oxford Dictionary of National Biography*. Oxford University Press.
"Linken-Politiker André Brie schwer verunglückt". Spiegel Online 06.03.2012. http://www.spiegel.de/politik/deutschland/kuenstliches-koma-linken-politiker-andre-brie-schwer-verglueckt-a-819766.html
Loades, David (1989): *Mary Tudor: A Life*. Blackwell.
Loades, David (1996): *John Dudley, Duke of Northumberland 1504–1553*. Clarendon Press.
Loades, David (2004): *Intrigue and Treason: The Tudor Court, 1547–1558*. Pearson/Longman.
Loades, David (2008): "Suárez de Figueroa, Gómez, first duke of Feria in the Spanish nobility (1520?–1571)". *Oxford Dictionary of National Biography*. Online edition.
Loar, Carol (2010): "Medical Knowledge and the Early Modern English Coroner's Inquest". *Social History of Medicine*. Vol. 23, No. 3. http://shm.oxfordjournals.org/content/23/3/475.short
Lovell, M. S. (2006): *Bess of Hardwick: First Lady of Chatsworth*. Abacus.

MacCaffrey, W. T. (2008): "Radcliffe, Thomas, third earl of Sussex (1526/7–1583)". *Oxford Dictionary of National Biography.* Online edition.
MacDonald, Michael and T. R. Murphy (1993): *Sleepless Souls: Suicide in Early Modern England.* Clarendon Press.
Maxeiner, H. and E. Ehrlich (2000). "Site, number and depth of wounds of the scalp in falls and blows – a contribution to the validity of the so-called hat brim rule". *Archiv für Kriminologie.* Mar-Apr. 2000. 205(3-4):82-91. http://www.ncbi.nlm.nih.gov/pubmed/10829237
Medscape: Imaging in Skull Fractures. http://emedicine.medscape.com/article/343764-overview
Murphy, C. P. (2008): *Isabella de' Medici: The Glorious Life and Tragic End of a Renaissance Princess.* Faber & Faber.
Murphy, John (2012): "The Royal Household of Mid Tudor England". http://john-murphy.co.uk/?page_id=1258
Murphy, T. R. (1986): "'Woful Childe of Parents Rage'": Suicide of Children and Adolescents in Early Modern England, 1507–1710". *The Sixteenth Century Journal.* Vol. XVII, No. 3.
Mystery Files: The Virgin Queen. http://natgeotv.com/uk/mystery-files/about
Neale, J. E. (1992): *Queen Elizabeth I.* Academy Chicago Publishers.
Nelson, Alan (2003): *Monstrous Adversary: The Life of Edward de Vere, 17th Earl of Oxford.* Liverpool University Press.
Parsons, F. G. (1929): "The Thickness of the Living Scalp". *Journal of Anatomy.* July. 63(Pt 4): 427–429. https://www.ncbi.nlm.nih.gov/pmc/articles/PMC1250069/
Pettigrew, T. J. (1859): *An Inquiry into the Particulars Connected with the Death of Amy Robsart.* J. Russell Smith.
Pollard, A. L. (1910): *The History of England from the Accession of Edward VI to the Death of Elizabeth (1547–1603).* Longmans.
Read, Conyers (1962): *Mr. Cecil and Queen Elizabeth.* Jonathan Cape.
Rye, Walter (1885): *The Murder of Amy Robsart: A Brief for the Prosecution.* Elliot Stock.
Simpson, Richard (1896): *Edmund Campion.* John Hodges.
Skidmore, Chris (2010): *Death and the Virgin: Elizabeth, Dudley and the Mysterious Fate of Amy Robsart.* Weidenfeld & Nicolson.
Statistisches Bundesamt (2017): "Todesursachen in Deutschland 2015". Fachserie 12 Reihe 4. https://www.destatis.de/DE/Publikationen/Thematisch/Gesundheit/Todesursachen/Todesursachen2120400157004.pdf?__blob=publicationFile

Templer, John (1992): *The Staircase: Studies of Hazards, Falls, and Safer Design*. MIT Press.
"Touristen-Insel Rhodos von Erdbeben getroffen: Eine Tote". Die Presse 15.07.2008.
http://diepresse.com/home/ausland/welt/398553/TouristenInsel-Rhodos-von-Erdbeben-getroffen_Eine-Tote
Tuchman, Barbara (1979): *A Distant Mirror: The Calamitous 14th Century*. Ballantine Books.
Virgoe, Roger (1982): "DUDLEY, Sir Robert (1532/33-88)". *The History of Parliament*. http://www.historyofparliamentonline.org/volume/1509-1558/member/dudley-sir-robert-153233-88
Weir, Alison (2008): *Elizabeth the Queen*. Vintage.
Whitelock, Anna (2009): *Mary Tudor: England's First Queen*. Bloomsbury.
Whitelock, Anna (2013): *Elizabeth's Bedfellows: An Intimate History of the Queen's Court*. Bloomsbury.
Wikipedia: Inch. https://en.wikipedia.org/w/index.php?title=Inch&oldid=766329210
Wikipedia: Kopfschwarte. https://de.wikipedia.org/w/index.php?title=Kopfschwarte&oldid=163240654
Wikipedia: Scalp. https://en.wikipedia.org/w/index.php?title=Scalp&oldid=787633644
Wikipedia: Skull fracture. https://en.wikipedia.org/w/index.php?title=Skull_fracture&oldid=782464003
Williams, Neville (1964): *Thomas Howard, Fourth Duke of Norfolk*. Barrie & Rockliff.
Wilson, Derek (1981): *Sweet Robin: A Biography of Robert Dudley Earl of Leicester 1533–1588*. Hamish Hamilton.
Wilson, Derek (2005): *The Uncrowned Kings of England: The Black History of the Dudleys and the Tudor Throne*. Carroll & Graf.
"Woman killed in Rhodes earthquake". Express 15 July 2008. http://www.express.co.uk/news/world/52534/Woman-killed-in-Rhodes-earthquake
"Young Women and Osteoporosis" (2014). CEMCOR. 14 April 2014. http://www.cemcor.ubc.ca/resources/young-women-and-osteoporosis-%E2%80%94-good-news-about-treatment-and-prevention

Index

Adams, Simon 119
Adlard, George 141
Aird, Ian 68
Álvarez de Toledo, Fernando, 3rd Duke of Alba 128
Anjou, Francois, Duke of 137
Anscombe, Allan 68
Appleyard, Henry 128
Appleyard, John 11, 20, 52, 56, 60, 109, 120–129
Appleyard, Roger 12
Auber, Daniel 140
Aylmer, John 15
Babington, Francis 61
Barthewe, Francis 98–99
Bayley, Walter 71
Becon, Thomas 11
Bigot, Anne, *née* Appleyard 26
Bigot, James 26
Blount, Thomas 44, 46–56, 61, 70, 75–76, 94, 96, 98, 100, 109, 110, 121, 125, 126, 130
Boleyn, Anne 42, 141
Bonington, Richard Parkes 140
Borgarucci, Giulio 99
Bowes, servant 46, 49–50, 62
Breuner, Caspar von, Imperial ambassador 33–35, 38, 72, 94
Buckner, Dorothy 42
Butler, Anthony 97–99
Butler, Charles 98
Butler, Mrs. 60, 97, 99
Camden, William 13
Campion, Edmund 61
Cave, Ambrose 101
Cave, Roger 107
Cecil William, Lord Burghley 13, 24, 25, 28, 80–88, 90, 104–109, 118–120, 122–123, 126–127, 129–130
Charles of Austria, Archduke 33–35, 37, 72, 118,122

Christmas, Robert 123
Clinton, Edward, 9th Lord Clinton, 1st Earl of Lincoln, Lord Admiral 88, 122
Coligny, Odet de, Cardinal of Chatillon 100
Cranmer, Thomas 19
Dee, John 29
Devereux, Robert, 2nd Earl of Essex 132
Devereux, Walter, 1st Earl of Essex 134–135
Donizetti, Gaetano 140
Dormer, Jane, Duchess of Feria 31
Doughty, Thomas 100
Douglas, Margaret, Countess of Lennox 100
Drake, Francis 100
Drew, Rose 68
Dudley, Ambrose, Earl of Warwick 12, 18–21, 24, 36, 80, 101
Dudley, Amy, *née* Robsart *passim*; accident 62–69, 89; burial 58–61; divorce 72; education 12, 140; and Elizabeth I 38, 77, 84, 85, 133; folklore 134–135, 138–139; grave 143–144; health 30–32, 68–72, 83, 120; historiography 140–142; injuries 65–66; letters 23–24, 45; in literature 138–140; murder 94–97, 100, 102–103, 108–109, 119–120, 123–124, 132, 136–137; murder investigations 46–58, 109–110, 122–129; in opera 140; personality 34, 35, 41–42, 77; portrait 142–143; possessions 17–20, 22, 25, 32, 40, 43–45; poison 33, 34, 70–72, 83; religion 11, 42; residences 11, 15–17, 21, 22, 31, 38–40; and Robert Dudley 13–15, 18, 19, 24–25, 29, 32, 35–37, 43–44, 77, 84, 118–119, 143; stairs 62–64, 66–68,

153

76–77; suicide 75–79; travels 29, 31–32, 43
Dudley, Andrew 21
Dudley, Anne, née Seymour, Countess of Warwick 13–15, 18
Dudley, Elizabeth, née Tailboys, Lady Tailboys 18
Dudley, Guildford 16–19
Dudley, Henry, conspirator 21, 39
Dudley, Henry, youngest son of the Duke of Northumberland 19–21, 24
Dudley, Jane, née Guildford, Duchess of Northumberland 15, 17, 19, 20, 70, 98, 125, 130
Dudley, John, Duke of Northumberland, Earl of Warwick 12–17, 38, 39, 75, 88, 89, 92, 94, 100–101, 125, 130, 133
Dudley, John, Earl of Warwick, son of the Duke of Northumberland 13, 18, 19, 101, 143
Dudley, Lettice, née Knollys, Countess of Essex, Countess of Leicester 100, 132–134
Dudley, Margaret, née Audley, Duchess of Norfolk 21, 31
Dudley, Margaret, daughter of Ambrose Dudley 25
Dudley, Robert, Earl of Leicester *passim*; letters 26–27, 46–48, 52–53, 55–56, 76, 80–81, 105–108, 117–118, 129–130
Edney, William 44–45
Edward VI, King of England 14–16, 61, 88, 94, 116
Enríquez de Toledo y Guzmán, María, Duchess of Alba 20
Elizabeth I, Queen of England 13, 16, 24, 27–31, 33–38, 46, 58, 61, 71, 72, 74, 77, 80, 82–94, 96, 99, 101, 113–117, 119, 120, 122, 125, 126, 128, 130, 132–137, 139–143
Eric XIV, King of Sweden 33
Ferdinand I, Holy Roman Emperor 35, 72, 118
Fisher, John 101

Fitzalan, Henry, 19th Earl of Arundel 35, 92–93, 122, 126
Flowerdew, Frances, née Appleyard 11, 12
Flowerdew, John 12, 23, 25–27
Forster, Anthony 37, 39–42, 50, 51, 54, 63, 78, 95, 98, 102, 110, 114, 130–131, 141
Francesco I, Grand Duke of Tuscany 137
Fraser, Antonia 119
Froude, James Anthony 84, 140–141
Garzia di Toledo, Leonora di 137
Gesualdo, Carlo, Prince of Venosa 137
Grey, Henry, Duke of Suffolk 16
Grey, Jane, *m.* Dudley, Lady 16–17, 19, 70, 116, 142, 143
Gunn, Steven 57
Guntor, Arthur 93
Hales, John 94, 102
Hastings, Henry, 3rd Earl of Huntingdon 73–74
Hastings, Katherine, née Dudley, Countess of Huntingdon 20, 21, 24, 74
Hatton, Christopher 132
Henry VIII, King of England 39, 61, 141
Herbert, William, 1st Earl of Pembroke 22, 122, 126
Hilliard, Nicholas 13
Hoby, Thomas 119
Horsey, Edward 123
Howard, Katherine 143
Howard, Thomas, 4th Duke of Norfolk 31, 32, 35, 109, 122, 123, 125, 126, 128
Huband, John 108
Huggyns, William, Amy Dudley's servant 29, 40–41, 43
Huggyns, William, John Appleyard's brother-in-law 120, 124–127, 129
Hugo, Victor 140
Hume, Martin 84
Hungerford, Agnes 136
Hungerford, Edward 136

Hyde, William 29, 38, 70, 77, 101
Il Schifanoya, Venetian ambassador 30
Jackson, J. E. 141
Jobson, Elizabeth, née Plantagenet, 18
John, Duke of Finland 33
Jones, Norman 95
Jones, Robert 89–91
Kett, Robert 12
Killigrew, Henry 89, 91, 133
Knollys, Francis 88
Lingard, John 140
Lucy, Thomas 105–107
Machyn, Henry 60
Manners, Henry, 2nd Earl of Rutland 32
Marlowe, Christopher 110
Mary I, Queen of England 16, 17, 19–22, 39, 61, 88, 123, 143
Mary Stuart, Queen of Scots 70, 99, 117, 119
Medici, Isabella de' 137
Messia, Marco Antonio 131
Mutlowe, Elizabeth 42, 60
Neville, Charles, 6th Earl of Westmorland 134
Noailles, Gilles, Abbé de, French ambassador 37
Norris, Henry 42
Norris, Henry, 1st Lord Norris 42, 56, 131
Norris, Margaret 42, 59, 131
Odingsells, Elizabeth 39, 41, 50, 63, 78
Orsini, Paolo Giordano, Duke of Bracciano 138
Owen, Anne 39, 41, 50, 63, 78
Owen, George 39
Owen, William 39, 41, 42, 131
Parr, William, Marquess of Northampton 32, 87, 88, 121, 122
Parry, Thomas 73
Parsons, Robert 61
Percy, Thomas, 7th Earl of Northumberland 134
Pettigrew, Thomas Joseph 141
Philip II, King of Spain 19, 20, 22, 31, 37, 69, 84, 115, 116, 131, 137
Picto, Mrs. 40, 50–51, 70, 75–76

Pius IV, Pope 93
Pollard, A. L. 141–142
Quadra, Álvaro de la, Spanish ambassador 32, 33, 62, 69, 72, 82–86, 91, 94, 115–116, 141
Radcliffe, Thomas, 3rd Earl of Sussex 46, 100, 122, 123, 125, 126, 128
Robersart, Chanoine de 11
Robsart, Arthur 11, 56, 109, 133
Robsart, Elizabeth, née Scott 11, 12, 14, 19, 22
Robsart, John 11, 12, 14, 19
Rye, Walter 141
Scott, Walter 36, 140
Seymour, Edward, Duke of Somerset, Lord Protector 12, 13, 15, 94
Shakespeare, William 106
Sheffield, Douglas, née Howard, Lady Sheffield 99–100, 135, 140
Sidney, Henry 17, 19, 31, 115–116, 135
Sidney, Mary, née Dudley 17, 20, 31, 80, 116
Sidney, Philip 71, 117
Simier, Jean de 137
Smith, Richard 55, 56, 113–114
Smith, Thomas 109
Steaphinson, John 115
Stevenson, Edward 56, 115
Stevenson, John 56, 114–115
Strong, Roy 142
Stuart, Henry, Lord Darnley 117, 125
Suárez de Figueroa, Gomez, 1st Duke of Feria, Spanish ambassador 28–31, 33, 69, 140–141
Talbot, George, 6th Earl of Shrewsbury 136
Teerlinc, Levina 142
Throckmorton, Nicholas 75, 87–90, 100, 117–118, 126
Tiepolo, Paolo 30, 69
Tryndall, servant 123–124, 127
Vere, Edward de, 17th Earl of Oxford 109, 137–138
Vere, John de, 16th Earl of Oxford 33
Verney, George 104–108
Verney, Richard 38, 95–108, 125, 140,

141
Verney, Richard, grandson of the former 104–108
Walsingham, Francis 117, 133
Ward, Edward Matthew 140
Webster, John 138
Weir, Alison 119
Whetell, Richard 61

Williams, John 97
Wilson, Derek 61
Wyatt, Thomas 19
Yeames, William Frederick 140

Made in the USA
Monee, IL
18 May 2020